THE BEST
LAW SCHOOLS'
ADMISSIONS
SECRETS

The Essential Guide from
Harvard's Former Admissions Dean

JOYCE PUTNAM CURLL

sourcebooks

Published by Sourcebooks, Inc.
PO Box 4410, Naperville, Illinois 60567-4410
(630) 961-3900
Fax: (630) 961-2168
www.sourcebooks.com

Library of Congress Cataloging-in-Publication Data
Curll, Joyce.
  The best law schools' admissions secrets : the essential guide from Harvard's former admissions dean / Joyce Curll.
     p. cm.
  Includes bibliographical references and index.
  1. Law schools--United States--Admission. 2. Law schools--United States. 3. Law schools--United States--Entrance examinations. 4. Student aid--United States. I. Title.
  KF285.C87 2008
  340.071'173--dc22
                              2008015094

Printed and bound in the United States of America.

POD 10 9 8 7 6

CONTENTS

To Dan

ACKNOWLEDGMENTS

Many people have had a hand in helping me get this project completed. Ted Fiske was a wonderful mentor, reader, and critic who encouraged me and provided guidance from inception throughout the writing of this book. Howard Gardner, Howard Seidel, and Dean Whitla offered encouragement along with help and ideas to make this project one that provides broader guidance than would a "step-by-step how-to book." Colleagues Ken Lafler, Anne Lukingbeal, and Dee Pifer provided helpful critiques and moral support, as did Marilou Blaine, Margaret Carlson, and Sue Milmoe, experienced professional writers, editors, and friends.

Numerous faculty members at Harvard Law School, including admissions committee members, have taught me and challenged me to be at my best throughout my time there. Some have specifically supported my idea to write this book, including Bill Alford, Alan Dershowitz, Martha Minow, Peter Murray, and Larry Tribe, and given me confidence to move forward on this project. I also want to thank my agent, Wendy Strothman, who has provided guidance in my new role as author, and Peter Lynch, my editor at Sourcebooks, for his enthusiastic support for this project throughout.

For the knowledge base from which I was able to write this book, I thank my colleagues from the Law School Admissions

Council, from the various prelaw advisor associations and from the admissions offices at Harvard and NYU who have served with me over the years in our joint enterprise of educating prospective applicants about the legal profession and encouraging them to enter it. I particularly want to thank Todd Morton, now Dean of Admissions and Financial Aid at Vanderbilt University Law School, who shared his knowledge and wisdom with me at both NYU and Harvard as did Nan McNamara who served with me at NYU and filled my position when I left for Harvard. I also want to thank Karen Buttenbaum and Sandy Williams for their great teamwork and support. Others who have been most influential in my education as an admissions professional include Dick Badger, Faye Deal, Rick Geiger, Ken Kleinrock, the late Jim Milligan, Jim Thomas, Jean Webb, Gerald Wilson, and Peter Winograd.

Most importantly, I thank my husband Dan, who provided moral support, encouragement, and sustenance, clearing the way for me to keep going.

INTRODUCTION

HAVING SPENT THE LAST eighteen years of a thirty-four-year career in law school admissions as the Admissions and Financial Aid Dean at Harvard Law School (HLS), I have considered for admission more than 120,000 HLS applicants, of whom about 10,000 applicants attended and graduated from HLS. More than 30 percent of the living alumni of the JD program at HLS were admitted on my watch. Before coming to Harvard, during sixteen years at NYU Law School, I considered another 100,000 applicants, of whom 6,000 became NYU Law graduates.

Throughout, I have had a wonderful window on society and particularly the world of current and recent college graduates, many of whom already had significant accomplishments under their belts and most of whom showed great promise for the future. And I have watched as those futures unfolded. Some students have flourished throughout law school and their careers. Some stumbled a bit before finding their feet; some enjoyed the law school experience, but not the practice; some hated law school, but loved the practice.

I have observed the whole range of possibility with respect to the experience of legal education and the profession. Many roads lead to law school, some direct and others circuitous. I have seen everything from the precocious eighteen-year-old college graduate and the twenty-two-year-old medical doctor who wanted to get a head start on the legal profession, to those who wanted to build on established, successful careers, like the fifty-something-year-old physician, the forty-something screenwriter who became president of the student body, and the forty-something engineer who became president of the *Harvard Law Review*.

You may be one of the many undergraduates who, seeking a livelihood after graduation, have been exploring the professions and, not liking the sight of blood and not having a knack for organic chemistry, have decided that practicing law would be an appealing way to earn a living. Perhaps you are one of those who tried investment banking or consulting and decided that law will get you where you want to be in a more intellectually stimulating and fulfilling manner. You may have been engaged in work that you enjoy, but see the value of a legal education as a stepping-stone to a more responsible position in the field in which you have been working.

If you are any of these, or are coming to a consideration of law as a career from another perspective, you are not alone in having some idea of what is involved, but still having questions about whether law school and the legal profession are right for you. You may be wondering how to proceed.

You are in good company. Even the strongest, most savvy applicants experience some uncertainty and more than a little trepidation as they set out. I have had ample opportunity to hear from many for whom the admissions process and legal education worked out the best. Most have told me that they wish they had had more understanding as they set out to apply: beginning with decisions about what to study in college, how to prepare for taking the LSAT, how to decide when and where to apply, and finally, where to attend once admissions offers were tendered.

Some of the more privileged applicants have access to experienced prelaw advisers and to friends who have navigated the process successfully, and even these still have questions. For those without this guidance, the admissions process can be daunting.

More than thirty years ago, I cofounded a group of admissions deans who designed a short panel discussion to impart our collective wisdom about the law school admissions process to prelaw students at our big feeder schools, and to gain insight into the applicant mind-set. Our panel discussion was designed to address misconceptions held by many potential applicants and missteps we collectively observed in the applications we considered. We addressed frequently asked questions in a coherent and organized way. I participated in this panel throughout my time at NYU and at Harvard. It worked wonderfully for applicants who attended, and our only frustration was that it was not possible to share it more broadly.

I have been inspired to write this book to share what I have learned from the students I have admitted, and some who were not admitted, about the anxieties and uncertainties they feel during the application process. Virtually all applicants, whether they have a knowledgeable prelaw adviser or not, feel somewhat bewildered or overwhelmed at times as they decide whether to apply, how to get started, what to emphasize, whom to ask for a letter of recommendation, what to say in a personal statement, and how to handle each step of the process. This anxiety and uncertainty is even more pronounced among students of color, women, those from non-college family backgrounds, those from immigrant families, and those from other groups not traditionally represented in the profession. By making the admissions process more transparent, I hope not only to provide guidance and reassurance to all applicants as you embark on this journey, but also to help level the playing field for those from groups whose access to advice and preparation for law school has been less than that of the average applicant. I hope to help all to get through the obstacle course, and many to the school of their dreams.

With the advent of the Internet, such innovations as chat rooms, threaded discussions, blogs, and the like give the appearance of providing broader access to advice about applying to and attending law school. The problem is that it can be very difficult to sort out good advice from bad. Much of what applicants tell each other in the chat rooms is bad advice. Blogs from admissions officers purporting to add transparency to the process have become just another way to market their schools.

I aim to provide you with sound advice from start to finish and to help you sort out the best from other information available to you on the Internet, in books, and in your personal interactions with prelaw advisers, admissions officers, and friends in law school or the profession. Even if you have had no interaction with these kinds of advisers, this book should provide you with guidance on reaching out to access an equivalent benefit.

This book is designed for you at whatever stage you are in your personal, academic, or professional development. After reading this book, you should be able to plan, refine, or explain your college experiences and achievements, as well as your employment experiences, to maximize your possibility of admission and your opportunities in preparing for the legal profession.

CHAPTER ONE

Is Law School for You?

LAW SCHOOL BY DEFAULT

Returning for his senior year, Ken came to the realization that this phase of his education would soon come to an end, and he would need to decide what to do after leaving college. It seemed appropriate to spring into action to fill that future void.

Ken was a good student who wasn't yet prepared for the work environment. The job market presented uncertainty. Fellowships and graduate schools would not be offered until spring term.

He quickly ruled out graduate work in his major field, because the job market for new PhDs was limited, and a master's degree wouldn't add much to what he could do with his college degree.

Staying in school seemed safe, and preparing for a profession seemed like progress. He had not taken enough science to consider medical school and business schools required a couple of years of experience before application. Law school was the only reasonable option. His parents were breathing down his neck about his plans after college and he needed to let them know that he was working on it.

Among other actions, Ken took the LSAT to see whether he was a viable applicant to law school. One out of five people he knew in his class were doing this, so it couldn't be a bad idea. He did pretty well and decided to apply to law school, like so many of his classmates. The law schools made it easy to fill out multiple applications, so he applied to several schools and by early spring, Ken had been admitted to a few of them. Hanging out in law school for three years put off dealing with the job market and kept his anxious parents at bay. He could continue to do what he had done well for the past few years—go to class, study, write papers, take exams, and live the life of a student.

Although Ken was not really sure he liked law school as well as college, he stuck it out. The school environment was comfortable and his teachers were dynamic, making the material interesting. He saw second and third year students going to class in their business suits and rushing around to interviews.

When he returned from his first summer, Ken found that employers were actually trying to persuade him to work for them. After being wined and dined by the big law firms, he eventually chose one where he thought he would enjoy working. The summer program involved interesting cases and frequent social activities. At the end of the summer, he was made a permanent offer by his firm, which he accepted. He started practicing law the following fall, after taking the bar and a short vacation.

THIS IS HOW MANY people end up in law school by default. Before Ken knows it, he may look back and realize that he has been practicing law for ten, twenty, thirty, or even forty years! He may wonder what would have happened had he taken a different path and landed in a different career. And all because he didn't want to address some hard questions during his senior year of college!

What happened to Ken is typical of many students, especially those coming directly from college. For some it turns out to be a good choice; for others it sets them on a track that will result in one more person unhappy with his or her profession. The expenditure of upwards of $180,000 (2007 costs) plus an opportunity cost of three years' salary, makes it harder to leave the profession. Income is important and student loan repayments loom.

The same path of least resistance that propels many to law school can keep them in the profession even when they might be happier doing something else. Because lawyers typically earn more than those in other professions, many continue to work in the profession despite dissatisfaction because of the investment they have made in their education and other preparation. They are responsible for their educational loans whether or not they continue in the profession, and the salaries they typically earn enable relatively easy repayment of loans as well as a lifestyle that it is difficult to leave. Just as Ken might have been better served by careful consideration of alternatives and of his own genuine interests, so most prospective applicants will benefit from serious examination and reflection.

LAW SCHOOL AFTER SERIOUS EXAMINATION AND REFLECTION

How do the most savvy potential law students decide whether to go to law school?

They follow most, if not all, of the steps below. They learn about themselves in the process, which helps them to make the most of their law school experience. With some extra effort at the front end, you can enhance your law school experience, or avoid it altogether. Do some research, talk to people in law school and the profession. Assess yourself and your own interests, and talk to more people before you take the plunge.

Research legal education

You can access information about legal education, about applying to law school, and about individual law schools at the Law School Admissions Council (LSAC) web site (www.LSAC.org). The LSAC is a nonprofit corporation organized by a group of law schools in 1947 for the purpose of developing and administering the Law School Admissions Test (LSAT). At that postwar time, there was a huge increase in applications to law schools, and the top schools were having difficulty deciding who should be admitted. (Throughout this book, as appropriate, I will refer to the LSAC and the services they provide through their operating arm, Law Services, Inc., using the two names interchangeably.) Having served on the LSAC Board of Trustees for five years, on the Board of Directors of the original Law Services during my time at NYU and Harvard Law Schools, and on standing committees and ad hoc committees for more than twenty years, I am personally aware of the good that LSAC has done for the benefit of applicants to law schools. The organization has worked tirelessly to enhance opportunities for applicants, especially those from groups who have been historically underrepresented in the legal profession, and those with limited financial resources to apply. They have helped make the entire process of applying to law school more transparent. All American Bar Association approved law schools and fifteen Canadian law schools, approved by provincial or territorial law societies or a government agency, make up the membership of LSAC.

The LSAC web site has links to all ABA approved law schools, and very helpful information about the services offered to applicants. Looking at each law school's web site is an excellent way to research individual schools to get a sense of what to expect in a law school.

Questions to address before applying

The most important question to address with respect to law school admissions is whether you really want to attend law school and enter the legal profession. This may seem obvious, but many otherwise organized and talented applicants have made no more than a cursory review of this question. Every year I come across seniors in college who are not sure what they want to do when they graduate. Some plan to look for jobs, apply to graduate or professional schools, and put off the decision about what they want to do until they have all their options in place. It is one manifestation of "senioritis." If you are a rising senior, and my earlier description of Ken resonates with you, or if it begins to do so when you return to campus for your senior year, you can begin anywhere but be sure to cover all the ground described below.

As you address this question, more questions will arise, including how your background and interests relate to the law and what aspects of the legal profession would make the best use of your background and match your interests and goals.

Research the legal profession

If you know nothing at all about the legal profession, you will want to understand how the legal profession developed. Aside from working in big corporate law firms, lawyers fill many roles. Some roles require a law degree; in others a law degree is not required, but is considered an asset. For example, to be a prosecutor, judge, administrative law judge, corporate in-house general counsel, or counsel to government, it is necessary to have a law degree. You might expect that to be a law professor one must have a law degree, but there are law professors with degrees in other fields that do not have a law degree. At Harvard Law School (HLS) there are two senior faculty members, outstanding in their fields, with no law degree. While not required to have law degrees, most arbitrators hold them; mediators need not have law degrees and many do not.

Other roles lawyers frequently fill include not-for-profit administrators, investment bankers, corporate executives, politicians, government administrators, and journalists.

To gain more insight into the profession, see the web sites for the HLS Program on the Legal Profession (www.law.harvard.edu/programs/plp), the ABA (www.abanet.org), and the Pro Bono

Institute (www.probonoinst.org). These web sites contain helpful information about some of the most pressing current issues for the profession.

Talk to those in the field

If you have access to lawyers and judges, talk to them about their work, or ask to shadow them at work for a day or more. Do your research in advance and you will get more out of your conversations and your shadowing experience. Not only will you ask better questions and get more useful information, but also you will be more likely to engage the interest of the lawyer or judge whose time you are taking. If the lawyer or judge has a specialty, find out as much as you can about it before your meeting, even if it does not hold special interest for you. The process will help you delve deeper into specialties that do hold special interest for you.

Watch a real trial

If you live in an area where it is convenient to visit a court, and to watch a trial or two, take advantage of that opportunity. If you are called to jury duty, consider it an opportunity to learn as much as you can about the court system and how a trial works. If you are empanelled as a member of a jury, you can see firsthand how the jury system works. If you have access to Court TV, watch a trial on TV—not just the highlights or the commentary, the whole trial.

Understand the influence of the media on prospective applicants to law school

One way that students become interested in law school and come to think they know something about it is through contact with the media. Many facets of the media contribute to the interest among young people in going to law school. From old reruns of *Perry Mason* to TV series of the '80s and '90s like *Ally McBeal* and *L.A. Law* to current series such as *Law & Order,*

Boston Legal, Shark, or *Damages,* students at top schools have shared with me that watching these shows has piqued or enhanced their interest in becoming a lawyer. Usually, they do not confess on their applications to being influenced by these shows, for fear that the admissions office will not take them seriously. Such an admission, without the proper context, might indeed put the admissions committee on high alert for signs that you have not seriously examined the profession.

Watching a movie or a TV show about lawyers and the law is not the best basis for developing an interest in law school, and many applicants for whom this is a prime motivator experience a rude awakening when they actually enter law school or encounter the reality of the practice of law. If your interest in the law has been piqued by the media, take further steps to examine the reality of legal practice.

Televised hearings of national interest such as the recent Supreme Court nominee hearings for Chief Justice Roberts and Justice Alito, the Watergate Hearings in the '70s, and the Clarence Thomas confirmation hearings in the '90s also have had an influence on applicants to law school. The first such televised hearings were the Army-McCarthy hearings of the early 1950s, and some of the most dramatic moments of those hearings took place in exchanges between the Boston lawyer Joseph Welch, the Army Counsel, and Senator Joseph McCarthy. Since these hearings represent actual events and conflicts, they also convey some understanding of how the processes shown actually work, and can be helpful to someone thinking about the profession even if there is a risk of glamorization.

ASSESS "YOURSELF AND THE LAW"

Some applicants have always assumed that they would go to law school, because their father or mother or some other relative did, and they haven't explored the idea in depth for themselves. Sometimes, as described above, they have been inspired by a

TV series where lawyers seem to be dealing with very exciting cases and leading glamorous lives.

Sometimes, like Ken, they are responding to parental pressure to think ahead about what to do with their lives, but without any clear idea how to go about that thinking. The idea can hit after you have tried a career other than law, been disappointed, and decided to look for something else. Whenever it hits, address the question of "you and the law" carefully before making the decision to apply.

So how do you assess yourself to see whether law school and/or the law is a good match for you? You want to find out about both in the course of your explorations. Explore law school for its own sake and as a component of whether you want to become a lawyer. Bear in mind that some people hate law school and love the practice of law, and others love law school and hate legal practice. Some love both and others hate both. Whichever you are, the exercise of exploration and self-assessment will give you a greater appreciation of what you are doing and why in your education and career. Without a serious prelaw assessment, attending a law school can be an expensive and time-consuming way to find that you do not want to be a lawyer.

You can take the steps below in an order that the opportunity presents itself or your inclination takes you. If you have become interested in the law by taking a course or a seminar, and there is a law school in your university or one nearby, visit a class to see how law is taught. You may also take advantage of the events that take place there, and the insights you gain from whatever you learn may help to inform your choice of courses or major in college. However you approach your exploration, each step will help you to make better use of the other steps.

Talk to law school representatives

Every fall, the LSAC sponsors large forums in major cities around the country. In 2007, they were held in Atlanta, Boston,

Chicago, Houston, Los Angeles, New York, San Francisco, and Washington DC. They include workshops on the LSAT, completing your applications to law school, financing legal education, and how to take the best advantage of talking to the law school representatives in attendance. Most member law schools attend, and typically thousands of prospective students go as well. The forums are especially helpful if you have been out of school for a while and do not have easy access to a prelaw adviser, and each forum is staffed with at least one prelaw adviser from the regional association of prelaw advisers. The forums also include panels of local attorneys engaged in practice, and panels of particular interest to minority, older, and nontraditional applicants.

The value of attending one of these events is that you can cover a lot of ground efficiently in a short period of time at one location. At the two-day forums, you can spend one day attending panels and another talking to law school representatives, or you can pack it all into one day. It is a good starting point for anyone interested in law school, including freshmen who are just beginning to think about law as a potential career.

In my own experience at forums, I have talked to high school students who were usually attending with their parents, and I always felt that I could help them think about a long-term plan to investigate the profession and legal education. I have also frequently talked with parents who were attending without their children, and found this a good opportunity to help the parents keep their role in their children's futures in perspective.

You can learn from the representatives at the least busy tables, even if you don't have a particular interest in their schools, remembering that at this stage you are learning about whether you want to apply at all, not where you want to go. They will give you very good answers to generic questions about applying, but be aware that they are also there to sell their schools. Beware of the representative who is actually a third year student or a recent graduate from the school, who has been hired to travel for the school for the season, but plays no other role in the admissions process beyond "selling" the school. Dubbed "McReps" by the full-time admissions officers, they are fine to talk with if you are interested in their schools, but otherwise not a lot of help and the possible conveyors of faulty admissions advice.

Beyond the forums, there are law school fairs sponsored by prelaw adviser associations, which are held at colleges and universities in various regions. Not as well attended by law schools, they have very limited or no workshops. You can find out where and when they are being held by going to the "Choosing a law school" tab on the LSAC web site. Click on "Recruitment Events" to see a map of the regions, which lists the dates and places. Those that are at the larger universities and are described as Law Days will have the most law schools in attendance. Do not travel very far to attend these unless you are particularly interested in a school or schools in attendance. Unless you are also interested in exploring other graduate school opportunities, you will be disappointed in the attendance by law schools at Graduate and Professional School Days. These are only worth your while if they are on your own or a nearby campus.

Visit a law school

Visiting a law school can be the first event triggering your interest and raising good questions about whether you want to go to law school. Although it is always best to visit a school in person, prior to any physical visit, you should visit "virtually."

The LSAC web site has links to all ABA–approved law schools, and very helpful information about the services offered to applicants. You can research a school in some depth before your physical visit. Visiting a number of schools in person can be very time-consuming at the stage when you are still deciding whether to apply. If there is a law school on your university campus, or one nearby, that can be the easiest one to visit in person. I will have more to say about how to maximize your visit when we get to the point where you are deciding where to apply and where to attend if admitted.

Attend recruitment events at individual schools

From each school's web site, you can learn about programs that might interest you. Many schools hold open houses and other events for prospective applicants during the fall recruitment season; most hold them for admitted applicants in the spring. Others hold frequent informal information sessions during the fall recruitment season. These events can provide opportunities for you to answer your own questions and to learn from the questions that other prospective applicants pose.

At HLS, I found information sessions helpful in a group setting because of the diversity of questions and the overall give-and-take. We paired an admissions officer with a student tour guide to host the sessions. After the session, the tour guide took the visitors on a tour of the campus, answering questions applicants were reluctant to ask an admissions officer.

In your search, check the school's web site for details of events and information sessions. You can also check their travel schedule for where else you might meet their representatives at your school or in your city. Many schools try to incorporate individual school visits into their recruitment programs. Check with your prelaw adviser if you have one, or with the Career Services office.

Attend law school admissions panels

An event to look for is a panel discussion of admissions officers. For many years, first at NYU and later at Harvard, I participated with colleagues from other top law schools in a series of panels that we presented at about twenty schools each year. We discussed the admissions process in general, offering shared opinions and advice on subjects about which applicants were frequently (or universally) concerned, and pointing out our varying views where we differed. We touched on highlights of our individual schools, using an "infomercial" format, and then answered questions from the audience. After each panel, we stayed around to talk individually with applicants who had more detailed or personal questions.

Other groups of schools adopted the idea of traveling together to present panels, although in different formats. Check web sites to see if any of these panels will be at your school, or at a school nearby. Typically, because of the format, the general public is invited to attend. The panels can be very helpful if you are an alumna/us or working in the area, since your access to other programs might be limited.

Talk to your school career counselors and prelaw advisers

If you are still in school or are working near your undergraduate school, talk to your prelaw adviser or visit your career counseling office to see what programs and advice they have to offer. Some prelaw advisers give an overview of the admissions process at the beginning of the year; some offer free courses to prepare you for the LSAT; some are astute about what schools might be a good match for your interests.

Those schools that have many applicants are best equipped to provide advice, although there are some egregious exceptions to this at some of the most elite schools, and often the big state schools have not allocated sufficient resources to support services for all prospective law students. Even if these schools have a knowledgeable prelaw adviser, that adviser can be overwhelmed by demand and may only advise people in groups.

Prelaw advisers come in two types. The first are faculty members, usually in the political science or government department, and their level of interest in the assignment will be reflected in how much advice they provide for your applications. Some will do an outstanding job for you, providing you with a recommendation and a push for you at the schools they think you should attend. Unfortunately, the advisers with those kinds of resources, knowledge, and credibility with law schools are rare.

The other type of prelaw adviser is the professional in the career services office. The smaller the office, the more likely it is that the prelaw adviser has responsibilities for other graduate and professional schools and/or employment as well, and will be less focused on law. This is good while you are still deciding whether law is for you, but less helpful when you are looking for more in-depth guidance.

However your school is staffed, there are some useful bits of information that you can ask for from your prelaw adviser. They have been through this issue many times, and may be in a position to help you think about important issues to address. More about this in the chapter titled Behind the Scenes.

Consult APLAs

APLA stands for Association of Prelaw Advisers and every region in the U.S. has one: the MAPLA (Midwest), NAPLA (Northeast), PCAPLA (Pacific Coast), SAPLA (Southeast), SWAPLA (Southwest), and WAPLA (Western). Loosely affiliated with one another through a national organization called PLANC (Prelaw Adviser National Council), they gather at a national conference every four years.

Peruse the web sites of the APLAs, bearing in mind that they have no staff and their web sites, managed by volunteers, are often limited and out of date. Bear in mind also that, while the prelaw advisers and the law school admissions officers are engaged in a mutual effort designed to benefit you as an applicant, and while they may enjoy good personal relationships with one another, there is also a natural tension, especially between the groups at large.

Prelaw advisers work hard to get their students into the best school possible and are frequently frustrated in that effort. From the individual law school's perspective, the prelaw advisers should direct their best students to attend the school they represent, and they are often frustrated in that hope. From a group perspective, the prelaw advisers work to keep the schools honest and the schools work to keep the prelaw advisers informed and evenhanded in their advice to students, and sometimes the shortfall in reality versus expectation creates tension between the groups.

Combine other interests or experience with law

Your interest in law might develop through seeing how it interacts with another profession or form of employment in which you are engaged either during the summer or after college. Revisiting the example of the media through a different lens, I have watched prospective law students come from the entertainment industry as screenwriters and assistant producers, and graduates go into the industry as entertainment lawyers, as well as screenwriters, producers, and the like. This is entirely different from being influenced by the media to practice law.

For example, Ed, whom I admitted to NYU Law School and who later transferred to Yale, is at this writing an executive producer for *Shark*. Prior to NYU, Ed studied at Harvard College, where he was involved in the theater; after law school, he brought his legal education together with those interests.

Alfredo, who was a member of one of my first classes at HLS, started his legal career in corporate litigation, but then cycled out to be a screenwriter, writer, and producer, and counts among his credits episodes of *Law and Order*. One of my favorite students, Voltaire Sterling, appeared as an actor in the movie *The Great Debaters* in 2007.

The quintessential example in this area of the law is Scott Turow, also an HLS alum, and author of nine books, three of which have been turned into films. Turow—whose first book, *One-L*, about a first year at Harvard Law School, was written during his first year at HLS—was actually a writer before he went to law school, having attended and taught in a creative writing program at Stanford University Graduate School. It is rumored that Turow had a contract to write *One-L* before he entered HLS. A great role model, Turow has engaged in the practice of law since graduation, first as a U.S. Attorney and then as a white collar criminal defense attorney in Chicago. He does pro bono work and numbers among his successes an appeal that led to the release of a prisoner who was on death row for a murder he did not commit (see www.scottturow.com/biography).

John Grisham, a lawyer-turned-politician-turned-novelist, and a graduate of University of Mississippi Law School; David E. Kelley, lawyer-turned-screenwriter-and-producer, and a graduate of Boston University Law School; and Senator Fred Thompson, lawyer-turned-politician-turned-actor-turned-politician, and a graduate of Vanderbilt University Law School all make great stories as well, although these have left the practice of law.

From another direction, Bill was a screenwriter in his late thirties. He was doing well, but he wanted more. He came to HLS, did well, and was a leader on campus. After graduating, he went to a law firm in LA, where he now practices law.

TEST AND ASSESS YOURSELF

Louisa Mattson, a psychologist at Essex Partners in Boston, shares her expertise working with high-level executives, including lawyers, to help them find good solutions in their search for a rewarding career. Her view is that any test or assessment of yourself should help you to understand yourself in terms of interest, skills, values, and style. If you can, take your first steps by assessing yourself. You may find that by doing so, you can direct your efforts toward those aspects of the profession that most interest you, where your skills will be put to the best use, your values honored, and where your style will be most effective.

An excellent first step to assess your own suitability to law school and the legal profession is to take a self-assessment test like the Myers-Briggs Type Indicator (MBTI). It may ultimately be of more value for you in getting you into law school than will a good score on the LSAT because, when you know yourself better, you can do a more credible job of presenting yourself on an application or in an interview.

The stereotype is that the best lawyer profiles are the Introverted, Intuitive, Thinking, Judging (INTJ) or the Extraverted, Intuitive, Thinking, Judging (ENTJ) individual. The qualities described for these types are often seen as lawyerly qualities, but one can find outstanding lawyers among all personality types. My own view is that taking the test will help you to focus on those aspects of the legal profession that are most suitable for your personality type. The legal profession is so broad that it has room for all personality types; the problem for many lawyers is that they end up in a part of the profession that is not a good match for them, just as in any choice made with respect to how you spend your working life.

Journal

Another approach recommended by Dr. Mattson is to keep a daily journal of the activities in which you engage, and how you enjoy them. Consider what appeals to you about the activity and why it appeals. Envision what components would be contained in an ideal job; imagine how you would like to spend your days (and sometimes nights). As you think about the kinds of lawyers you have come to know, what lawyers do you admire and what do you admire about them?

Live the question of being a lawyer. What are relevant lifestyle considerations and what difference do they make to you? Writing your thoughts over a period of time can help you focus on what is most important for you personally and professionally. Knowing what you like to do can help you in your search for the right career. Writing on a regular basis will enhance a skill that is important in law.

Intern and find employment

Get an internship with a lawyer, a law firm, or a judge so that you might have the opportunity to see what they do on a daily basis. The same advice about being prepared for talking with a lawyer or judge holds true here. Be forewarned that working as an intern or paralegal might or might not be helpful to you, and recognize that you might just find yourself copying documents or performing other simple repetitive tasks without actually coming into contact with the lawyers. The more knowledgeable you are, the more likely they are to give you more responsibility. If you have this option, try to find out how much access you will have to the lawyers in performing your daily tasks. You may find that a smaller law firm will give you more varied tasks and closer interaction with the lawyers. The more responsibility you have and the more able the lawyers are to observe your work, the more likely that a letter of recommendation from them would be both substantive and useful in your application to law school.

If you have an interest in a career in nonprofit or nongovernmental organizations, look for an opportunity to work in a nonprofit organization, to see how lawyers operate in those environments. Recognize that these are some of the hardest jobs to come by, and often the least well paid. They might only be able to offer you an unpaid internship. If you can afford it, a reason to take such an internship is that previous experience in this area can demonstrate your commitment to public service on your application and help you if you are looking for a job in public service after graduation from law school.

If you want to gain practical insight into how laws are made, look for an opportunity to work as a congressional intern, or in your state or local government. You might learn more about politics than the law, but you will see how laws affect individuals or groups in the real-world.

If one opportunity that fits your criteria shows up before another, take it. There are several kinds of explorations you can and should do as your "due diligence" review of whether law school and a legal career beyond is right for you.

Even if you find yourself engaged in very mundane tasks to support the work of the office, make the most of it, watching carefully what your superiors are doing to understand the content of the work and their daily routine. Remember that learning about the profession is your primary goal.

ALPHABET SOUP: KNOW YOUR LAW SCHOOL ADMISSIONS ACRONYMS

The application process for law school introduces a new vocabulary. Each new term or acronym represents a facet of the process. Some represent services that provide benefits to you directly and indirectly through the schools. The schools benefit from many of the services described, saving both time and labor and having more information at hand to make quicker, fairer decisions. Familiarizing yourself with the terms and acronyms, the services provided for you, and the tools used by the law schools can help you with the steps you will need or want to take. Understanding the information to which the schools have access as they evaluate and compare your application to those of others can help you in your own presentation.

LSAT

The LSAT is the best known acronym, standing for the Law School Admissions Test that virtually every applicant must take to get into law school. See the chapter devoted to the test for everything you want to know about it. The people who bring you the test are the LSAC, or Law School Admissions Council, the organization made up of all the ABA (American Bar Association) approved (accredited) law schools as described above. The ABA requires use of a test in the admissions process at all accredited schools, and the LSAT has been the test used by the schools.

LSAC and LSDAS

The LSAC also has created an organization known as Law Services, Inc., which provides many services to you the applicant, and to the schools. The LSAC web site (www.LSAC.org) is a treasure trove of information and data that you can use to learn more about the law school admissions process generally and the law schools individually and collectively. Because it is a membership organization, the LSAC steers completely clear of evaluating schools or making any statements that will prefer one school over another. It is not the best place to find advice that distinguishes schools from one another, or that ranks them. Each school has an equal say in decisions made by the LSAC.

The LSAC created the LSDAS (Law School Data Assembly Service), which collects transcripts from your undergraduate and graduate schools, and provides a summary of your undergraduate transcript or transcripts along with a copy of the transcript to the law schools. This is a tremendous service for you, because you need send only one transcript for each school you attended to the central clearinghouse at Law Services, and they will analyze them, summarize them, and send them to every law school on your list.

This is also a beneficial service to the law schools because, instead of getting loose transcripts from each of the schools and analyzing and summarizing all those transcripts themselves, they receive a neatly assembled packet for each applicant along with the transcripts attached and a summary sheet with the grades calculated by year, summarized, and converted to a 4.0 system. They combine this information with the LSAT score report and, where the schools request it, provide an "index" that gives the schools information predicting your first year grade average, a surrogate for potential success in their school. (See the chapter on quantifiable factors for further information on the subject.)

To verify and validate this information, schools submit first year grades for their entering classes at the end of their first year, and a "validity study" is performed to determine the degree to which performance in the first year correlates with the prediction made during the admissions process by combining grades and scores.

Because the LSDAS is a national service, used by all law schools and required of virtually all applicants, it is also the data source for a host of reports and other services provided to you and to the schools. Those services and reports are outlined below. For more detail and further discussion, see the chapter on quantifiable factors.

CRS (Candidate Referral Service)

When you sign up for the LSAT, you can choose whether or not you are willing to be contacted by schools. Schools can search for you using demographic data available in the LSDAS database, including your age, year of graduation, racial or ethnic identity, state of residence, undergraduate school, grades, and LSAT. Schools can use the search mechanism to target students they hope to attract, sending viewbooks, CDs, and other materials to encourage you to apply, plus invitations to open houses

Tuition Deposit Overlap Reports

For years, the law schools struggled with an issue that made it difficult to control the size of the entering class and the related delay in notifying wait-listed candidates of their chance for admission. Many admitted applicants, reluctant to make the difficult choice between schools until the last minute, would hold places in as many as three or four schools. Schools could not fill slots from the wait-list until a vacancy occurred. The result was "musical chairs" and some chaos in the late summer virtually every year. Law schools tried returning part of the tuition deposit at periodic points in the summer, to jiggle loose applicants sitting on the fence, but this had limited effect.

After years of frustrating efforts to solve the problem without violating individual applicant privacy, the national response to the problem was the creation of the deposit overlap report. On a regular basis from late spring throughout the summer, schools submit the names of the admitted applicants who have paid tuition deposits or statements of intention to enroll to a central clearinghouse at Law Services. In return, schools receive a report indicating how many of their deposited students have also placed deposit at which other schools. Knowing how many students and where else they have deposited helps schools make judgments about making offers to the wait-list. To protect applicant privacy, no information about individual applicants is provided.

If you are on a wait-list at your school of choice, the final decision on your application may be expedited because of the existence of these reports. You can help relieve the overall problem by narrowing your own choices among your admission offers to one school while you sit on the other wait-list. Your good citizenship may help break the logjam, and could help open up a place for a student who is holding one at the school *you* most want to attend.

Tuition Deposit Overlap Reports

For years, the law schools struggled with an issue that made it difficult to control the size of the entering class and the related delay in notifying wait-listed candidates of their chance for admission. Many admitted applicants, reluctant to make the difficult choice between schools until the last minute, would hold places in as many as three or four schools. Schools could not fill slots from the wait-list until a vacancy occurred. The result was "musical chairs" and some chaos in the late summer virtually every year. Law schools tried returning part of the tuition deposit at periodic points in the summer, to jiggle loose applicants sitting on the fence, but this had limited effect.

After years of frustrating efforts to solve the problem without violating individual applicant privacy, the national response to the problem was the creation of the deposit overlap report. On a regular basis from late spring throughout the summer, schools submit the names of the admitted applicants who have paid tuition deposits or statements of intention to enroll to a central clearinghouse at Law Services. In return, schools receive a report indicating how many of their deposited students have also placed deposit at which other schools. Knowing how many students and where else they have deposited helps schools make judgments about making offers to the wait-list. To protect applicant privacy, no information about individual applicants is provided.

If you are on a wait-list at your school of choice, the final decision on your application may be expedited because of the existence of these reports. You can help relieve the overall problem by narrowing your own choices to among your admission offers one school while you sit on the other wait-list. Your good citizenship may help break the logjam, and could open up a place for a student who is holding one at the school *you* most want to attend.

End of Year Overlap Reports

The end of the year overlap reports were developed to help schools plan their marketing and to expedite the selection process. In return for submitting admission and matriculation data on all admitted applicants, and a promise to keep the information they receive confidential, the schools receive a report that shows the overlap with every other law school with respect to applicants, admitted applicants, and matriculated students. They can see who their competition is with respect to all of these and plan their recruiting efforts accordingly. The reports can become controversial when some schools assert claims about how much they are preferred to another school based on the report. When a school violates the confidentiality agreement, the competing school is sometimes forced to defend itself, and that can violate the same agreement.

Prelaw Adviser Action Reports

When you signed up for the LSDAS, you could express a willingness to have your admission information sent to the prelaw adviser at your undergraduate school. If you did, they will receive a report on what happens to your application at all the schools to which you have applied. As an applicant, you can request information from that same prelaw adviser about applicants who applied in prior years. To protect their privacy, and yours after you have applied, there is no individually identifiable information available to applicants, but the general information can help you compare your own credentials to those who preceded you in the application process.

Misconduct Reports

These reports are generated to notify all schools affected as a result of misconduct or misrepresentation by an applicant. Misconduct can be anything from cheating on the LSAT to forging a transcript or letter of recommendation, misrepresenting involvement in extracurricular activity, or any other act or omission that intentionally misrepresents you as an applicant. Any school to which you apply can "catch" something on your application that they regard as misrepresentation and send it to the Misconduct Committee of the LSAC for investigation.

If you are charged with some form of misrepresentation, you will be given a chance to defend yourself and to respond to the complaint. If you are found guilty of misconduct or of misrepresenting information in your application, the finding of the committee will be sent to all law schools to which you have applied, and to all law schools to which you might apply in the next several years.

The moral: be totally honest in your representations about yourself. Don't even consider any violation. With that many schools watching, very little will get past them.

Forums

The LSAC sponsors the major forums held in major cities around the country, as described in the section on getting ready to apply. These forums cost you only your time and your travel expense, while the law schools pay a registration fee to participate.

Forum Summary Reports

Each year, LSAC sends to each law school a report on the forums held the previous year, providing demographic information about those who attended the forums, including information about those who applied to law school that same year. Specific to the school receiving the report is information about the number and demographic information of those who applied, were admitted, and matriculated at that law school. Law schools can use this information to perform a cost-benefit analysis on the utility of participating in each forum. Some schools attempt even more specific information on their own, by asking applicants to fill out forms for their individual schools.

After each forum, schools can order mailing labels for all those people who filled out information forms as they entered the forum. Sometimes that information is used to send you follow-up information or invitations to events.

Publications

The LSAC publishes materials that can help when you take the LSAT and choose among law schools. They include the *ABA/LSAC Official Guide to Law Schools*, and copies of previously administered and disclosed tests. You can take the test under conditions approximating actual test conditions and then score it for yourself. One publication explains the item types on the test and the logic behind the correct answers.

Electronic Application

The LSAC provides a means for filing your application to all your chosen schools electronically. When you sign up for LSDAS, you will be given the option of filing your applications to the individual law schools electronically. Some law schools require that you file electronically, others prefer it, and virtually all accept electronic applications. By submitting information commonly used along with individualized information required by each school, attaching your personal statement and resume electronically, and paying the individual application fees through LSDAS, you can file all your applications at once.

Letter of Recommendation Service (LORS)

Another service offered for convenience to applicants and law schools is a Letter of Recommendation Service. Applicants can print a form to give to their recommenders, who can send their own letter to Law Services, which in turn sends to the law schools designated. Letters can be general and sent to all schools or targeted to a particular school. This saves you, your recommenders, and the schools time and effort.

FINAL THOUGHTS

If you have done your research; assessed yourself; talked to law schools, lawyers, and prelaw advisers; asked your questions and listened to the answers from all your advisers; and gained some firsthand experience; the decision about whether to apply will become more clear. You may still have some uncertainty, but you will have addressed those questions that are basic before moving to the next phase. Understanding law school admissions lingo and the tools used by the admissions pros will help you put your best foot forward if and when you do apply.

CHAPTER TWO

When Should You Go to Law School?

IF YOU DECIDE THAT law school is for you, when should you plan to go?

If you take the advice of countless law students, you will take at least a year off between undergraduate college and law school. Almost universally, students I've known who came to law school directly from college tell me that they wish they had taken some time off between college and law school. Those who took time off are always glad and report how much more they got out of law school because of it. Nevertheless, about 35–50 percent of an incoming class enters directly from college, depending on the job market for college graduates that year. Of these, some worked before college, or during time taken off from college. For some of them, taking no time off between college and law school may work out fine. For most of those who came straight to law school, however, the rush to law school makes it harder to get the most out of the law school experience. The lack of sustained work experience or time in the "real-world" means that you bring less perspective to your studies and you may have lower tolerance for the more tedious aspects.

If you have had ample opportunity to explore the profession through summer internships in college and part-time work experience throughout college and you know a number of lawyers, judges, and law professors, you may miss out on less when you start directly out of college. Ironically, most people in this position see the value of taking time off to get more insight into the profession and the world at large.

If you are determined to press on and apply directly from college to law school, observe some added precautions related to the application process. Since you will apply with only three years of grades, or two if you are in such a hurry that you are graduating in three years, be sure to send in your first term grades as soon as they are available. Stay engaged with your application and send in any new information about your academic record as soon as it is available. This includes first semester grades, thesis results, and any information about graduation with honors or election to Phi Beta Kappa. The more of your record you can include, the more you resemble those who have been out of school for a while.

Even after you have been admitted to law schools, consider whether you want to go right away, or whether the benefit of working for a year or so will help you to get more out of your legal education. Most law schools will grant deferred admission upon request to at least some of their admitted applicants.

TAKING TIME OFF BETWEEN COLLEGE AND LAW SCHOOL

Taking time off between college and law school is an antidote not only to "senioritis," but also to academic burnout that many recent college graduates experience. Taking one to several years to work before making the decision to apply has many advantages and very few drawbacks other than the obvious one of delaying the start of your legal career. One incidental advantage to your application is that your complete college record is available to the admissions committee. Since senior year is often the strongest year (but not always, so don't expect admissions committees to assume it), your chances for admission improve with just that additional boost.

Depending on how you spend your time away from school, you may have some valuable real-world experience to add dimension to your credentials. You will do yourself a service if you take the time to do something other than academics before you apply. Real-world work experience can also help you in the job market when you enter your legal career or it might come in handy down the road of that career, when you specialize. Work experience can also provide partial compensation for a less than wonderful academic record. Don't expect that one year of experience will do all this for you, but several years of experience with increasing responsibility and skills developed can make all the difference!

ADVANTAGES OF EMPLOYMENT

The more experience you have of any kind, the better equipped you will be to take advantage of the law school experience. Although any kind of experience will help, the experience of working in a paid employment office setting has added benefits. Working in a paid position after you graduate from college provides financial resources and a sense of control over your finances and your life. It may be your first time living on your own, away from family, home, and college dormitory, your first real period of adulthood.

Most jobs will dictate at least a partial schedule of your time. You will get up earlier than you did in college, and spend a solid block of time at work each day. An important benefit of working is developing an understanding of the office environment. You may be offered an opportunity to work from home. Although this may seem attractive in some respects, it can be isolating and you will miss the experience of the office environment.

Having developed some control over your finances and your time, organizing yourself for school will seem easier.

When you return to academia, even if you have enjoyed working, you will have a greater appreciation of being back in school, and you are more likely to be efficient and effective in tackling your studies.

Finding employment

Getting a job out of college is dependent on a combination of your previous accomplishments, your academic experience, your summer work experience, your connections, and just plain luck. Luck relates primarily to what the overall job market for undergraduates is like when you graduate. In good years, the career services offices at the top schools are besieged by employers like investment banks, consulting firms, corporations, and the like.

In recent memory, there have been lean years when these employers have been interested only in the crème de la crème of college graduates. In a particularly lean recent year, many employers withdrew offers already made when the need for new employees dried up completely. The next year, they were back besieging the career services offices. Not surprisingly, the lean years yield many more law school applicants directly from college.

Regardless of which hiring environment describes your job hunting year, you may find that the path of least resistance is not the one that best prepares you for your future career. This time can be one of the best in your life to experience the job search with few negative consequences to your overall well-being and with the prospect of some wonderful discoveries.

What kind of work is best?

_____

Jim was a college graduate who, when contemplating law school, decided that working as a paralegal in a big law firm would be the perfect way to spend the time between college and law school. His dad was a lawyer and could help him get such a job with his firm. Jim figured that such work would boost his application to law schools, by showing his interest in law. His experience would also help him when he got to law school and to get a job after he graduated.

Most of my colleagues in law school admissions would agree that for Jim, as for most law school hopefuls, this could not be farther from the truth. If he thought that this experience would distinguish him from the pack, he would be sadly mistaken, because paralegals are a dime a dozen in the law school applicant pool. The idea that it would help him in law school was stretching the value of the work experience. Such experience might help him for the first month of law school, at best. The likelihood that it will help him in the job market three years hence is slim. Let's look at another example.

Jane grew up in a blue collar family. She had no relatives who were professionals, let alone any relatives or friends who were lawyers. She became interested in the law while majoring in political science, but she still was not exactly sure what lawyers did from day to day. Her senior year, she looked hard for a job that would give her some insight into what lawyers do. When she saw a listing in her career services office from a law firm looking for paralegal assistants, she decided to apply. She accepted the job they offered after she learned that she would be part of a group of paralegals that met biweekly to learn about the big issues in the cases on which the firm was working. She figured she could learn more about the profession in the job than by just reading about it or making appointments to talk to some local lawyers.

For Jane, the same job has much more value added than for Jim. Without working at the law firm, she would have had no real opportunity to understand directly what a legal career might hold. For Jim, working as a paralegal added nothing. He got the job through his dad, who was a lawyer and had been talking to him about the law since he was a young boy. Jane didn't know any lawyers, and her whole concept of what lawyers do came from her studies and from television series. Seeing the inside of a law firm as an employee benefits her for the particular purpose of deciding whether or not this is a profession she wants to pursue. She showed initiative in seeking out the position. For Jim, taking a job as a paralegal showed no initiative, it was just marking time between college and law school.

If your background is like Jane's, working in a corporate law firm may make sense, and is the easiest job of this type to find. The structure of these firms depends on having a number (the larger the firm, the larger the number) of paralegals to do routine work supporting the work of the attorneys. If your background is like Jim's, you should seek employment outside the legal profession or in some aspect of it that is different from the law firm.

If Jim were more adventuresome, he might reap more reward by seeking a position in a nonprofit organization in some way related to the law, or in a government agency or legislative office. He could work for a judge, a district attorney, or an attorney general to see how justice is done. If he were interested in learning about law in different settings from what he already knew, he could work for a nonprofit and see law in action, if indirectly. Such work can also provide insight into operations at the kinds of organizations that are beneficiaries of pro bono work.

A better way to spend time between college and graduate or professional school is to explore careers related to law and those other than law. If your background is like Jim's, choosing "other than law" might uncover unexpected synergies between what you choose and your legal career. You may develop some important skills and gain valuable experience that will help in both your legal education and career. Some highly remunerative positions of this nature include work in an investment bank, a consulting firm, or as an engineer or a computer expert. Less remunerative is work as a journalist, a teacher, and nonprofit work generally.

You may find an opportunity that builds on your interests developed in college, both through your academic work and your extracurricular experience. If you take the time to explore options other than law-related work, the worst case is that you may find a career that suits you better than law.

How is work valued by law school admissions committees?

Admissions officers and committees value work experience as they consider your application for admission. They value it both for its content and for the maturity that you gain from it. Only one law school (Northwestern University) actually comes close to requiring it at this writing, but almost every law school considers it a plus when evaluating your application. I will discuss the nature and value of different kinds of work in greater detail in the section on qualitative factors in the selection process.

ADVANCED SCHOOLING

Other common ways for applicants to spend time after college before applying to law school are attending a graduate program or taking some graduate courses. Unless this work is in a professional program, it is not ordinarily different from the work you did in college, and therefore the benefit is marginal. There may be good reasons for you to consider undertaking some graduate work between college and law school. The best reason is that you have a passion for the subject you intend to study. In this case, doing graduate work at this time will serve you well, as it will be much more difficult to undertake this kind of schooling after law school. For a career as a law professor, a PhD in such fields as philosophy, economics, and the sciences, among others, can help you get a position at a top law school. The top schools in recent years have increasingly looked for an additional advanced degree, particularly the PhD, for their new faculty hires.

If you seek a professional degree that is often associated with the law degree in a joint or concurrent program, you should wait to apply to both schools in order to reap the benefit of the relationship between the two programs. You can usually save a year of schooling, between the two programs. This can be true of the PhD as well, so you might check into this before you are too far along into your PhD coursework to take advantage of it.

Undertaking advanced academic work can sometimes help to overcome some weakness in your academic record, particularly if you are in a demanding academic program requiring sustained research and rigorous study. However, if your reason for taking on graduate work is solely to mitigate the effects of a weak undergraduate record, you may be spending your time unwisely. Graduate programs in liberal arts are heavily grade inflated, and it is difficult to distinguish the average from the outstanding.

TRAVEL, FELLOWSHIPS, AND INTERNSHIPS

A wonderful way to spend time between college and law school is to travel and see the world. One special way to do this and to enhance your application to law school is to win a traveling fellowship or a fellowship that takes you to another country to study. If you should win one of the national fellowships that are quite rigorous in their selection process, you will also get a leg up on the law school admissions selection process, even at the most demanding schools. The most selective fellowships are recognized as such by those involved in selective admissions programs at law schools and winning one of them is tantamount to a glowing letter of recommendation.

Included among the most prestigious post-college fellowships are the Rhodes and British Marshall, which are very competitive and involve studying in England. The Fulbright can take you any number of places, and the Watson Fellowship is an opportunity to follow your passion around the world. The Coro Fellowship program is a unique way to experience a variety of professional sectors in the U.S. over the course of a year. There are numerous other fellowships given to graduates of particular schools by their schools. Check with your career services office to see what your school offers.

Some other programs to consider include the Peace Corps, Teach for America, and Americorps' City Year (founded by two HLS grads) or VISTA. Programs like these provide an opportunity to be of service and to get to know people from different cultures, different socioeconomic backgrounds, and/or different segments of society within a framework that facilitates a learning component. They will also set you apart from the average applicant and enhance your chances of admission.

If travel is one of your interests and you do not find an opportunity to undertake it through an established fellowship or program, you can travel on your own or with friends. Although many students have a study abroad experience under their belts by the time they graduate, some do not find the time to do it either during the academic year or in the summer. The time between college and graduate or professional school may be one of the last opportunities for you to undertake this kind of experience before entering the professional world. If you can afford it, take a year and simply travel, seeing the country or the world. If you need to work to support your trip, spend a few months working prior to the trip, saving as much as you can, or you can find work in some of the countries to which you will travel. Many students who studied abroad in college will take the opportunity to build on the experience they had in college.

FINAL THOUGHTS

Whether you work, study, or travel or some combination of these during this period of your life, make it something that has meaning for you. You will always be glad you took time for it, and it is the best way to assure that your experience will have meaning for the admissions committee.

CHAPTER THREE

Preparing Your Case While You Are in College

PLANNING AHEAD

THE MOST IMPORTANT ACCOMPLISHMENT you can achieve in college is to find your passion, or at least something you are passionate about. The most valuable aspect of the college record for applicants seeking admission to schools like Harvard and NYU is not the grade point average or even the overall academic record. The applicants I have admired most have chosen their majors to suit their interests, taken rigorous courses in and beyond their majors, and integrated their extracurricular and work experiences with their academic experiences. They have developed valuable skills from each aspect of their educations in and out of class; and even more through the integration of their experiences.

Most importantly, they found at least one thing they loved to do and/or to study. To paraphrase the words of one great Harvard Dean to the Freshman class, "While you are in college, it is important to learn a little about a lot of subjects and to learn a lot about at least one." (Dean of the Faculty of Arts and Sciences Jeremy Knowles, in his annual welcoming speech to the freshman class)

If you are presently in college, you can still make choices that will maximize the value of your college education. At whatever point you are in your education, you can develop a plan going forward. If you have already graduated, you can still think through how what you have done to date can be understood, enhanced, and explained when you file your law school applications.

A good resource for this aspect of your preparation is a book entitled *Making the Most of College*, by Richard J. Light, who for many years led the Harvard Assessment Seminars, involving faculty members from some twenty-five colleges and universities. The group undertook research to evaluate the effectiveness of university teaching and find ways to improve it.

Among other things, they learned that extensive reading, with questions in mind about the reading, enhanced understanding and mastery of the material, and that effective writing was a key to success.

Law schools also find reading comprehension and writing, along with analytical reasoning skills, to be the most important abilities to develop in preparation for law school and the practice of law. Admissions committees routinely look for evidence of these skills.

In talking with law students, I have found that much of what Professor Light has found works in the college environment works as well or better in the law school environment. If you are still in college, developing these skills can not only help you maximize your undergraduate academic experience and enhance your chances for admission to the best law schools, but also equip you to handle the work in law school. If you have already graduated, analyze what your experience did for you and do what you can to develop these three most important skills further. As admissions committee members evaluate your application file, they will be looking for evidence of these skills in your transcript, in letters of recommendation, and in your personal statement.

DEVELOPING THE NECESSARY SKILLS

Reading, writing, and analytical skills might be the most important and the most basic, but are by no means the only skills you will need. Other skills valuable to lawyers include interviewing, investigation, research, problem analysis, counseling, active listening, negotiation, project management, time management, and advocacy, which all have a basis in reading, writing, and/or analytical reasoning.

Light and his colleagues found that students' understanding was enhanced when the teacher included study questions to guide their reading.[1] Reading skills are essential to any academic endeavor. Pleasure reading comes in all sizes and shapes, from short story fiction to long nonfiction books. Whether you read for pleasure or for class, practice reading with your own questions in mind. It keeps you engaged and improves your comprehension.

Another Light finding was that reading courses involving one-on-one discussion with a faculty member were among the most rewarding for students.[2] Even if you read for pleasure, plan to discuss what you are reading with others. Form study or discussion groups with fellow students in your reading courses. To help with your analytical, active listening, and advocacy skills, prepare to argue one side or another, or both sides of any given issue about which you are reading.

Reading extensively will also help you with your writing. One of Professor Light's graduate students surveyed graduates many years out of school and found that 90 percent ranked the "need to write effectively" as a skill of great importance in the work they were doing at the time.[3]

In studying Harvard College students, Light found that 83 percent of undergraduate students wrote more than 60 pages of final draft writing each year. Long research papers and writing for one's peers were some of the best motivators for students to strengthen their writing skills.[4] To help you develop and refine these skills, try to incorporate enough writing in your academic work to complete at least sixty finished draft pages per year. Get specific feedback on your writing, either from your teachers or from your peers and rewrite based on the feedback you receive. If your school offers writing tutors on campus, you may want to take advantage of their advice, even if you don't feel the need for remedial help. Although you may be told that you write perfectly well and have no need of their services, you may also get some valuable pointers.

While you are working on your writing skills, don't ignore the need to build your analytical skills. If you have extensive work in social sciences and humanities, be sure to have some courses that require you to work with numbers. Mathematics and other quantitative courses are the best ways to improve your analytical skills. Philosophy, usually considered to be part of the humanities curriculum, can help develop reasoning skills and integrate reading, writing, and analytical reasoning skills. Interdisciplinary courses can help you learn to synthesize ideas from different disciplines.

CHOICE OF MAJOR

As you consider how to develop your skills for law school, it may seem that you should choose a major that will help you in law school, or to get into law school. Do not allow the idea that you might wish to attend law school to dictate your choice of major. No one major is best to help you get into law school. Most incoming law students have majored in political science, government, or some other social science. However, these majors may not be the best ones for *you* to choose if you know you want to go to law school. No major prepares you better than others for law school itself because the preparation for law school is more the acquisition of skills and learning how to learn than the subject matter content of any one major.

Some majors that appear particularly geared to preparing you for law school, such as prelaw, business, communications, rhetoric, and the like, are actually particularly suspect as lacking in academic rigor and balance. The classic liberal arts or science majors are considered better, because of the broader range of knowledge they provide and the skills they will help you develop.

For example, literature is good for developing reading and writing skills, while philosophy can integrate those with analytical skills. Mathematics was the major of the great constitutional scholar, Larry Tribe, who teaches at HLS. People trained in computer science—and the sciences in general—are in demand in the intellectual property and patent law areas of practice.

The most important consideration when you choose a major is whether you are really interested in the content. It is your interest, not the content, that matters. Keep in mind the skills you are developing from each course, rather than the subject matter, both within and outside of your major.

Choosing a major can help you along the way to finding your passion. If you love what you are studying, the likelihood is that you will perform well. It may also help you to understand better why you want to attend law school or what aspect of the law interests you the most. Admissions committees may be more interested in you because you have majored in something different from those who have taken a more standard route. When you graduate from law school, you may find that your undergraduate major helps you find the employment opportunity that best fits your talents and interests. This is especially true for those who have majored in math, science, engineering, environmental studies, computer science, and the like.

COURSE SELECTION

When you choose your major, plan to balance it with courses that expand your understanding and enhance your skills. For example, if you choose the sciences, mathematics, engineering, or even economics, choose some courses that expose you to literature and require you to write. If you are a political science major, expose yourself to mathematics and/or some science courses, as well as literature. If you are a literature major, take courses in math, science, economics, and government or political science. Taking at least a basic course in philosophy will be valuable no matter what you major in.

Get beyond large introductory courses early in your academic career. It may be necessary to take some large courses later on, but participation in smaller courses will help you develop better study habits. Smaller classes will help you develop skills and habits like good listening and speaking, staying current with your reading assignments, and engaging with the material being discussed in class. Take seminars, or at least courses that meet in small groups, as it is more likely that you and your fellow students will be more actively engaged in those classes. Do this as early as freshman year.

Select your courses for the interest they hold for you and for the skills you will develop, especially if you are inclined to be a more passive recipient of knowledge. In your larger classes, don't be a back bencher, particularly one who is multitasking and letting others take a more active role. You will learn much more if you put yourself in the best position to stay actively engaged. Whenever you can, take courses that require your active participation. Active participation in a class which encourages it will not only help you to get a better grade—you will also learn more.

Light describes a "one minute paper,"[5] where at the end of class, the professor asks the students to write brief comments about the big idea that came out that day, and about what was the main unanswered question that remained after class. Both teacher and students learn from this. Try it yourself in all your classes. It will keep you alert and it will also help your writing skills.

Don't just listen to the teacher; listen actively to the comments that other students make and be prepared to make a response, even if you don't actually respond every time. Active participation in college classes will prepare you well for your law school classes, which typically require this of you. In law school, you will learn as much from your classmates as you will from your teachers and your books. And the same thing can be true of college!

Look for courses that require teamwork with your fellow students to complete at least some of the assignments. The opportunity to learn from your fellow students will enhance your academic experience and help you to prepare for law school. One of Professor Light's findings[6] in looking at students who were in academic difficulty was that almost all of them always studied alone. Studying alone deprives you of the chance to hear what others think about the books you are reading and about the ideas with which you are wrestling. It also deprives you of the chance to try out your own ideas and reactions on others. Working with others will prepare you better for how law school is taught and studied; and how you will practice law after you graduate.

EXTRACURRICULAR AND COMMUNITY ACTIVITIES

When Harvard Law School undertook a self-study as part of a strategic plan a few years ago, the researchers found that students who were actively engaged in extracurricular or community activities, or work such as research that took place on campus, were significantly happier than those not involved. Professor Light found the same was true of undergraduate students in his research.[7] He also found that those who were actively engaged in out-of-class activities did about the same academically as those who were not. Those who were involved in extracurricular or voluntary activities and paid employment also performed similarly. There was no significant relationship between the level of involvement and grades, but there was a clear relationship between participation and satisfaction with college. Even those with very heavy outside involvement did not do significantly less well.

The only place where Light found a modest but negative relationship was between the hours spent on sports and grades, but here he found some of the happiest students.[8] On another "performance" front, the arts, including music, dance, and especially drama, often helped to make connections between in-class work and outside activity. Making connections between your experiences in and out of class, and finding synergies between the work you do in class and your extracurricular activities, is likely to enhance both your experiences and your performance.

Extracurricular and community activities help you become a well-rounded person, and to develop qualities and skills that will be valuable to you in law school and beyond. Every member of the admissions committees with whom I have worked, and every law school admissions colleague whose opinion I value, considers extracurricular and community activities an integral and very important part of the picture when considering a candidate for admission.

WORK EXPERIENCE AND INTERNSHIPS

What is true of extracurricular activities and volunteer work in college is also true of paid work. Most students, especially those on financial aid, must work to help finance their educations. The undergraduate students at Harvard who work average seven to twelve hours of paid employment per week. Work that takes place on campus will add to your satisfaction with your college experience.

In the financial aid office at HLS, we hired undergraduate students to help us with our clerical work. Those students were glad to understand another part of the university and enjoyed helping other students. Some of them went on to careers in financial aid or some other aspect of student service in an academic setting, and some of them went on to law school. All of them were happier with the college experience as a result of their work experience there.

Other undergraduate students I have known have been able to find work as research assistants to faculty members in the arts and sciences or at the business school. Some have even found opportunities to do research for law school professors.

Students who have done very well in subjects like mathematics, economics, and the sciences have had the opportunity to become teaching assistants in undergraduate courses. Your knowledge in subject areas like economics, mathematics, computer science, and the sciences will help you become a research assistant or teaching assistant.

HOW TO MAKE THE MOST OF YOUR COLLEGE EDUCATION IN AND OUT OF CLASS

To prepare yourself for success in our rapidly shrinking and changing world, you will find it critical to develop a mind-set to help you navigate this world throughout your career, taking advantage of your relationships with people very different from yourself in background and perspective. Make every effort to interact with students from backgrounds different from yours, from different parts of the country, and from other countries. There may be times that it seems uncomfortable to reach out, but college and law school are among the safest places to explore differences. They provide an environment where you can use what you have in common with people from other backgrounds to get to know them, learn from them, and begin to understand their different perspectives and points of view.

Along these lines, take advantage of any opportunity to study abroad. Every year, roughly 200,000 Americans study in foreign countries. The language skills you gain and the experience of living in a foreign country will be valuable for law school. Even if you do not have a specific interest in international law, much of corporate practice has an international component to it simply because of multinational corporations.

If you have a large class, form study groups with others from your dorm. Plan to meet as a group before dinner at least once a week, letting your discussion spill over into dinner. Although everyone should do all the reading, consider dividing up the reading assignments for the week so that each of you comes prepared to lead the discussion for some portion of the work.

If you have the option, get involved in outside activities and/or work that is located on campus. When you find an activity or work that you enjoy, stay involved in it long enough for it to advance your skills. College is not like high school, where you might have been involved in just about every activity even if at a low level.

I have always been drawn to applicants who had really committed to a small number of activities and grown to leadership positions, developed skills, or took their organization into new initiatives that lead to very interesting experiences. They are more attractive than applicants who could list dozens of activities in which they were only a limited participant.

If you are struggling in any way, ask for help. Talk to your teachers and other advisers. You are not alone, and not the first person to experience what you are wrestling with, nor are you the last. There are people ready and willing to help. You may even, at a later time, help another student with similar issues. What you learn about yourself and about the value of seeking help when you need it will translate into managing the law school admissions process more effectively, and will help you make the adjustment when you begin law school.

Stay current with course assignments, prepare before class, and take the time to think about what you are learning so that you can take advantage of the professor's office hours to advance your understanding of the material beyond what is in the reading and in the classroom. Doing so might open an opportunity to serve as a research assistant on a project of interest to you. If you do this kind of preparation with several of your courses, you will be well situated to ask a faculty member to work with you one-on-one in a reading course.

Whatever else you do, follow through on what interests you most in your courses and in your activities and you might just find your passion!

MAKING EFFECTIVE USE OF YOUR SENIOR YEAR

Suppose you do not pick up this book until your senior year. There is still time to make adjustments and take advantage of my advice. Review your record and your transcript to see what you have done that follows my advice, and if there is anything new to do to help you in your senior year. In particular, see whether there are any courses or types of courses that you have not yet experienced that would help develop your skills. If you are like most students, you will find areas that could use some improvement. Most find that more writing is of value.

If nothing else, this might be a good opportunity to try something completely new, outside your comfort zone. You might want to try an extracurricular activity that interests you, but for which you haven't yet made time.

HOW TO ANALYZE YOUR OWN RECORD WHILE YOU CAN STILL MAKE CHANGES

What are you looking for when you examine your transcript? I will discuss this in more depth in the section on the quantifiable factors, to which you can turn to help with your examination. For now, consider whether there are any gaps in your education or whether your selection of courses is well balanced between quantitative courses, reading and writing courses, courses both in and outside your major.

- Have you taken any risks?
- Do you have areas of study where you didn't do that well but think you could do better now?
- Are your courses "rigorous"?
- Do you have many pass/fail courses?
- Can you show some substantial research and writing accomplishments? Do you need to do more reading? If so, what areas would be of interest and/or of value to you?
- Have you developed your writing skills to a point where you are comfortable writing when you need to express yourself? If not, consider taking a course that will require you to write a lot.
- How about your quantitative skills? If you need to work on these, find a course that will help develop them.

Ideally, you will have done this exercise each year before you sign up for the next year's courses, but it is worth a reminder, since reexamining the big picture on a regular basis can get lost in the urgency to fill requirements for your major, your minor, or your core requirements.

CHAPTER FOUR

Preparing Your Case: The College Graduate with Experience

I F YOU ARE A college graduate with some work experience under your belt, there is good news for you, depending on what you have accomplished since you graduated. As described previously, additional academic experience can sometimes help to mitigate weakness in your undergraduate academic experience and add a level of expertise to your academic record. This experience is particularly valuable if it relates to a passion you have developed or to long-term goals for your professional life.

Employment can help you in a number of ways. It, too, can mitigate some weakness in your undergraduate record by demonstrating ability and skills. And it can provide a record of experience in the real world to add to your academic experience, providing dimension to you as a person, a potential student, and an emerging professional. Law schools like to see paid employment as part of your experience. The kind of work that you undertake can be of great value.

More important for both endeavors is how you handle the academic or work environment, whatever your specialty or your job, and what you learn, both about the substance of your work and about yourself as a future professional.

ADDITIONAL ACADEMIC WORK

If your record is very strong, your application will benefit from your employment regardless of how much time elapses between college graduation and when you apply.

If your academic record is less than stellar, its impact on your admissions chances diminishes as your record recedes into the past. The more time you put between you and that record the better, depending on how you use that time. Redemption is hard to come by, but the admissions committee will be more likely to forgive some weakness in your record if you present a strong LSAT. The role the LSAT plays is more important as the years out of school pass, which is good news if you do well on standardized tests, but not so good if you do not.

How to improve your chances of admission after you have graduated from college

How can you improve your chances of a good outcome on your application?

First, reread the section on preparing your case throughout college. Consider what you have done consistent with the recommendations in that section, and what more you can do to build your record, both academically and out of class. Make sure the good things that you have done do not get lost as you prepare materials for your application.

For example, if you found a mentor, be sure he or she is one of your recommenders, even if he or she has left the university since your collaboration. If your grades showed a strong upward trend, was this because you only came into your own senior year, or was it because you were in the wrong major in your first year or two? If you are the classic late bloomer, you are among the few who might benefit from taking some graduate courses, to demonstrate that the end of your undergraduate record was not a fluke.

But, if your only reason for undertaking graduate work is to mitigate a less than stellar undergrad record, do not undertake it as a full-time student unless you have a very strong interest in the subject for its own sake. Otherwise you may expend great effort for something that has little impact. It would be far better to take on full-time employment and to seek to continue to develop quasi-academic or alternative skills to balance your academic record.

If you decide to add more academic work to your arsenal of achievements for reasons beyond mitigating your academic record, choose the most rigorous school and take the most challenging course possible, setting aside enough time to allow you to perform your best. Since law school admissions committees might not know that much about the school where you are taking the added classes, do what you can to inform them, especially if the grading system at the school is rigorous. Such information is more credible coming directly from the school. Once you have completed the coursework, ask your teacher for a recommendation pointing out the rigor of the course and your level of performance compared to that of your classmates.

Unless you intend to pursue the subject to a doctoral level, law schools are unlikely to dramatically change their impression of your academic ability or achievement. Further, you are unlikely to be admitted to a strong PhD program unless your record has particular strength in the field you intend to pursue.

Even earning a PhD can cut two ways. The PhD requires extensive research, writing, and expertise in a particular field. If you contemplate a career in law teaching, it could be an ideal building block. A PhD might just put you in the "expert" category, and demonstrate the kind of academic performance that can completely obliterate even a poor undergraduate record. On the other hand, if you go directly from college into a graduate program, graduate with the PhD, and apply directly to law school, you run the risk of looking like a perpetual student, a candidate looked upon with skepticism, unless the field is particularly in demand by law school employers.

PAID EMPLOYMENT

For most people, full-time work has many benefits for your impending law school application. The experience of being a part of the workforce, getting up at a regular hour, and going into an office every day will provide some insight into what it means to be a professional and earn your own living. Following a daily schedule will develop habits to better organize your time when you return to school. Understanding what it means to work for a living will give you an appreciation of your education when you are in school. Many returning students treat law school as a full-time job with extra activities that are related. If you take your job seriously, you may develop habits that will help you make the most of law school.

What kind of employment lends itself well to the time between college and law school?

There are many different alternatives, and the best advice I can give is analogous to what I said about choosing a major in college. Do what you love, or at least what holds interest for you, if you can find someone to pay you to do it, or even if you can't. Law schools look for a wide range of people with varying backgrounds and skills. Working at something "outside the box" will help you stand out in the applicant pool.

Choose a job that allows you to continue learning and developing skills that will help you in law school. Some examples include research analysis, financial analysis, journalism, teaching, or work with a management consulting firm. A job that gives you experience with analysis, writing, negotiation, research, presentation, and/or public speaking will help you with law school admissions, your law school experience, and the profession.

Even if you find only one of these attributes in your job, you can improve your chances and your skills. Any customer service or sales job will help your negotiation skills. Working as a research assistant to a writer or frequent public speaker can help you learn about communication skills.

Avoid the temptation to take a job that allows you to work from home. Working in an office is an important part of the learning experience for pre-professionals. Not only will you benefit from the discipline of the office environment, you may also benefit from the opportunity to work on a team that is engaged in some project or other. The teamwork skill will be important for you throughout your legal education and your career.

UNPAID AND "MENIAL" WORK

What if you can't find a "good" job? Especially in those lean years discussed earlier, you might not find a position that helps you develop any of the skills mentioned above. You might only find a position that seems quite menial. If so, you have two options:

1. Seek an unpaid internship or voluntary position in hopes of gaining better experience, more interesting work, and a better chance at any paid positions that become available in the organization.
2. Take the menial job and use the opportunity to learn about the people for whom that job might be a stretch. Understanding how they think and what is important to them might help you to understand your clients or a jury in your later career. It will also provide you with respect for people who have been less fortunate than you in their educational opportunities, but who have a strong work ethic and great common sense!

Either choice holds the possibility for enhancing your professional understanding and skills. Consider either choice as part of your educational experience and apply the principles described in the section of preparing your case while you are in college.

If you choose the former, treat it as if you are being paid. Work just as hard, take it just as seriously, and be just as reliable as a volunteer as you would be if you were being paid very well. Take each task you are given and do it to the best of your ability. Seek guidance from your supervisor when you need it, and keep notes so that you don't have to ask the same question twice. But ask again if you are not sure that a new situation is the same as the one you asked about before.

Work on any of the basic skills mentioned above. Take advantage of any opportunity to work on a team. Observing how a team works has value, working on it has more. Chances are that you will be given increased responsibility and maybe even a paid position if you are lucky enough to be there when one opens up.

If you choose the latter, or it chooses you, use it to understand people whose backgrounds and whose lives are different from yours. You might find it hard to break down a barrier with you on the other side as the "college kid." Work just as hard as they do, help them out when they need it, and respect them for what they are and what they bring to their work; you will learn a lot, and gain their respect and friendship.

With a positive attitude apparent, you will also gain the respect of the admissions committee for the qualities you display through this experience. Remember that lawyers are involved with real-world activities and real-world clients. The more experience you have throughout the range of society, the better prepared you are when it comes time to practice law.

Another option you could consider if you need the money that a paid position provides, but your heart lies in another direction, is to take the paid position that is offered, but also volunteer part-time in a position where your heart takes you. The time it takes might interfere with your social life. On the other hand, it might actually provide a rewarding social life because of the opportunity to work with others on something that really interests you. The admissions committee will respect your need to earn money and admire your determination to follow your passion.

THE OLDER APPLICANT

Applicants who are older than the average are attractive to admissions committees, depending on the breadth and quality of their academic, work, and life experience. The maturity and experience that they bring to the class often adds dimension to the educational experience of their classmates. What makes you an "older" applicant?

It is difficult to quantify what makes someone an older applicant, but generally he or she has five or more additional years of life experience than the average college graduate. In most cases, this also means about five or more additional years of work experience than the freshly minted graduate, even if he or she is in fact a freshly minted graduate. This could be work experience before matriculating at college, or full-time work while attending college part-time.

Law school differs from college in the range in age and experience of the students. I have seen everything from eighteen-year-olds directly out of college and twenty-two-year-olds who have completed medical school to people in their mid-fifties who have been engaged in other careers that led them to law. One was a widow who had worked with her lawyer husband throughout his career and who sought the degree to legitimize taking over where he left off. She was a wonderful, active member of the law school community, and a great role model for the younger students.

Most students in law school are in their twenties and early thirties, ranging from freshly minted college graduates to experienced professionals in fields other than law. Applicants with different levels of experience are at different points on the spectrum of personal development.

For each applicant, the moment of application is a snapshot in time, a point in personal development with some accomplishments and potential for the admissions committee to evaluate. The immediate college graduate has more accomplishment than the high school senior, but less than the work experienced graduate. For those lower on the spectrum of development, potential for success is more important than for those farther along on the spectrum, where actual accomplishment replaces potential.

The older the applicant, the more accomplishment there should be to consider. If you fall into the category of "older" applicant, the admissions committee will expect to see accomplishment in whatever you have done. If you are applying to law school because you are disappointed in your career path to date, you have a burden of proof to persuade the committee that you are suited to the law. If you have enjoyed your past work or career and have found that a law degree would help you to achieve a new goal, or if there is a logical transition to law in your accomplishments to date, you have made the best case.

Legal education, and particularly the Socratic Method of teaching, thrives on experience of students.

In a Criminal Law class at HLS, Professor Rich was describing what the police might do in a particular situation. Steve raised his hand and said, "I don't think the police would take that particular action." Professor Rich taunted, "Now, who in this class even knows a policeman, let alone what he or she would do in this situation?" "I do. I was a detective in Houston for the past twelve years."

Laughter erupted. After all, how often do you get to see a Harvard Law School professor taken by surprise? The laughter subsided when Professor Rich, not missing a beat, peppered Steve with pointed questions. Steve became a class expert on law enforcement, Professor Rich demonstrated how useful the Socratic Method can be, and Steve's fellow students learned that at least one classmate added something special to the class.

Most students can contribute something of value to the class, though not always as dramatically as Steve. The best teachers use their students' experience and expertise as teaching aids. Whether that experience is in medicine, banking, law enforcement, teaching, social work, sports, or Internet start-ups, it can add value to the class. Older applicants, especially those with substantial work experience, are of great interest to the admissions committee and to their law school teachers.

Each year, I reported to the dean and the first year faculty information about the incoming students to help the faculty learn some of the special experiences and areas of expertise that students brought to the class. The wealth of their combined experience prior to law school was always gratifying and portended an exciting learning environment.

Some of the special qualities beyond specific achievements and expertise that older applicants bring to the class include maturity, focus, leadership skills, people skills, speaking skills, writing and language skills, analytical skills, and decision making skills.

With some experience under your belt, you may be wondering whether to request a letter of recommendation from an employer. My answer is that it is appropriate once you consider your work experience to make a major contribution to your application. Whatever employment you take on, it can be just as important to find mentors as it was when you were engaged in your academic career; maintaining a network of fellow workers and supervisors can help when you need a letter of recommendation for law school or help in finding your next job.

FINAL THOUGHTS

Taking time out between college and law school will help you in your law school applications and will help you in your work in law school as well. Thinking in advance about how each possibility will help to develop your interests, your skills, and your understanding of people will facilitate your decisions and prepare the arguments you will make as you present your case to the law schools. Remember that it is not so much what kind of activity you engage in as how you engage in it.

CHAPTER FIVE

The Law School Landscape

WHEN YOU APPLIED TO college, there were literally thousands of options to consider: large universities, small liberal arts colleges, engineering schools, business schools, communications and journalism schools, arts and performing arts schools, community colleges, technical institutes, and so on. Having had a myriad of choices at the college level, it may surprise you to know that there are fewer than 200 accredited law schools from which to choose.

When you applied to college, there were only a few dozen schools that admit less than half their applicant pool. But most law schools admit less than half of those who apply.

The population of law schools overall in 2007-08 was more than 140,000 in JD programs, with about 49,000 new students that year, drawn from an applicant pool of about 84,000.[1] This is tiny compared to the roughly two million applicants to college each year. Still, even with the relatively small number of aspirants, the demand for legal education outstrips the number of spaces available by a greater percentage than does the demand for college education for spaces in college. The fact that law school is the gateway to a prestigious profession accounts for demand at virtually every school. All accredited law schools deliver the education required to prepare for the profession.

So what difference does it make where you go to law school? Let's have a look at some of the ways in which law schools vary and what some of the alternatives are.

HOW ARE LAW SCHOOLS ALIKE AND HOW DO THEY DIFFER FROM ONE ANOTHER?

Law schools are different from graduate school in general and from other professional schools. But compared to each other, law schools are more alike than they are different. The basic legal education varies primarily in the quality of your teachers and your fellow students. Each law school will provide you with a good legal education and equip you with the tools to enter the legal profession and practice law.

The curriculum in the first year of law school is pretty much the same at virtually all law schools, consisting mostly of required courses, including Civil Procedure, Contracts, Criminal Law, Property, Torts, Legal Research, and Writing.

In the upper class curriculum, a few courses are required at some schools and strongly suggested at others. Even with the basic courses, some schools will focus on helping you develop breadth and depth in understanding the law and legal reasoning.

Since law schools prepare you for a profession, the perspective of the legal employer on law schools is important to consider. Because of employers' preference, some law schools will provide you with a myriad of opportunities in law school and beyond; others will provide you with enough opportunity to satisfy most of your needs; at still others it will be necessary for you to make your own opportunities.

The law schools differ from one another in size, location, specialized programs, quality of the educational experience, diversity of the student body, quality of life, and where their students can expect to be employed after graduation. Considerations such as location, size, and special programs may be important to you while to others they may not matter. Some differences have subjective components to them because of personal preference.

For example, what for one person contributes positively to the quality of life may for another person be a reason to avoid the school. Attending law school in a rural setting may be for some the last chance to live in the countryside before beginning an essentially urban profession. For others, a rural setting may feel too isolated and out of the mainstream. For some students, a larger size represents a broader opportunity and a chance to work with people who share even your esoteric interests; for others, it seems impersonal and anonymous.

HOW IS LAW TAUGHT AND WHY IS IT TAUGHT THAT WAY?

One similarity among law schools is how law is taught, which is different from what happens in college and other graduate and professional schools. In medical school, students dissect a cadaver as part of the learning experience; in law school your teachers will be teaching you a new language and turning your mind inside out to teach you to think critically and dispassionately about cases and issues. (Visiting a law school class is a good way to observe the training that lawyers have been through.)

The old saying that "the first year, they scare you to death" has a kernel of truth to it. The first year of law school is like going to a foreign country where you don't speak the language and trying to engage in daily life along with the locals. The sooner you pick up the language, the easier life will be. To learn the language of a foreign country, you need to practice it regularly. The same is true of learning "legalese." It takes daily practice, persistence, and patience.

Most faculty members use the Socratic Method, which involves a dialogue between the faculty member and students about cases that have been decided at the appellate level. These traditional teaching methods have been used without dramatic change for more than a hundred years. How well the Socratic Method is done is important to its utility.

Done well, it involves a well-guided discussion of the case, the issues it raises, and the applicable doctrine and legal principles. Teachers make use of hypothetical situations to mine the material. These are an important feature of the Socratic Method, involving slight changes in the facts of a case and sometimes taking hours in class teasing out resulting changes in other aspects of the case. Hypotheticals help teach the student how to think critically about issues, judicial reasoning, doctrine, and legal principles when considering other cases. Done poorly, or by a mean-spirited faculty member, the Socratic Method evokes a caricature out of *The Paper Chase*,[2] harassing and humiliating the unfortunate student who has been called upon "cold" to give the facts of the case and to work through the issues it raises.

The best of legal education combines the development of critical reasoning skills with training in their practical application. Aspects of legal education that bear some resemblance to medical education are clinical courses and skills training. Clinical training is called "live client" learning because the fieldwork component includes live client representation. Clinical courses at their best add experiential understanding and structured practical training to the academic understanding that students gain in their more traditional classes. At worst, they provide experience from which you can learn on your own from mistakes that you and others might make, with no reassurance about whether you have learned the best way to handle a similar case.

Other courses, like trial advocacy and negotiation, have a simulation experience or skills training as a supplement to—or a substitution for—the fieldwork experience.

WHAT KINDS OF LAW SCHOOLS ARE THERE?

Some of the differences among law schools relate to the nature of the work toward which each school's graduates are headed, and some relate to the nature of the individual school's academic scope and setting. Law schools are categorized as national, regional, local, "niche" schools, independent, and unaccredited. Some schools fit more than one of these categories.

National law schools

The so-called "national" law schools are considered the top schools. They are likely to focus on legal analysis and jurisprudence rather than on state law or preparation for the bar exam, which all law school graduates must pass to become members of the bar and licensed to practice. If you graduate from a national law school, you will be better equipped for—and more likely than students from other schools—landing a job in a major law firm, a clerkship with a federal judge, a clerkship at the U.S. Supreme Court, and/or a law teaching position.

What makes these law schools national is that their applicant pools and student bodies are drawn from across the nation and around the world, and their graduates disperse as broadly at graduation. Each has a sizeable population from other regions, more or less according to the size of the population in those regions, although some may draw students a little more heavily from their own region.

For example, as perhaps the most national law school because of its size and reach, Harvard Law School's largest state representation for most of the past several years has been California, followed by New York. In years where California is not the largest, it is second to New York. Home state Massachusetts has a sizeable representation, but significantly behind that of the most populous states. NYU's largest representation is New York, not surprisingly, because New York is one of the two most populous states and also the home state for NYU.

Although most of the national law schools are private, four or five state schools lay claim to national status, including University of California at Berkeley (Boalt Hall), University of California at Los Angeles (UCLA), University of Michigan, University of

Texas, and University of Virginia. If you are from the states of California, Michigan, Texas, or Virginia, you have a better shot at being admitted to a state school that is also national in scope. Public schools are likely to draw more heavily from their home states than do the private national schools, partly because of state requirements to have a certain percentage of "in-state" students, but will still have a national appeal.

Competition for places in the national law schools is intense. If you hope to attend one, you should have a strong academic record, do well on standardized tests such as the LSAT, have a strong record of extracurricular and community activities, and write well. National law schools place their students in the larger cities across the country, again a little more heavily in their own region. HLS places about as many graduates in California as it draws students from California, but sends quite a few more to New York than come from there, because of the many very large law firms located in New York City. NYU looks more like a local school, as does Columbia, because of their very high representation in New York.

The preponderance of the graduating classes from NYU and Columbia locating in New York is also the reason that average salaries reported by graduates of these two schools are the highest in the country. The combination of being national schools but local to New York City results in mutual attraction between them and the big law firms. The national schools outside of New York send graduates to New York but also to other major cities to a greater degree, with lower average salary and cost of living.

National law schools are sometimes dubbed the fifteen to twenty "top 10" law schools, because fifteen to twenty schools claim they are among the top ten schools in the country by some measure or another. Those which are virtually always included in the top ten according to most knowledgeable observers are (in alphabetical order): Columbia, Harvard, NYU, Stanford,

University of Chicago, University of Pennsylvania, and Yale, as well as Berkeley and Michigan from the public side. Other contenders include Cornell, Duke, Georgetown, Northwestern, University of Southern California, and Vanderbilt among the private schools, as well as UCLA, Virginia, and Texas from the public side.

Regional law schools

Regional law schools are at the next level. Most of the state law schools not in the fifteen-plus "top 10" fall into this category, and they typically dominate their region if there is no national school located in or near their state. If you are not a candidate for the top law schools, or you are a borderline candidate, you will probably gravitate to a law school in your own home region or the region in which you hope to practice. A state school may well be your top choice.

Employers tend to look for new lawyers first from the national schools, then from the regional schools within their own region. As a graduate from one of these law schools, you will find it easier to find a job within your region rather than outside; although if you graduate at the top of your class, you may have a broader choice.

The regions, using the descriptions defined by the Law School Admissions Council, are (in roughly clockwise order) Northeast, Midsouth, Southeast, South Central, Mountain West, Far West, Northwest, Great Lakes, and Midwest.

Although the fundamentals of what is taught at the regional schools are essentially the same as the national law schools, more of the examples used in class will come from state law, from that of adjacent states, or the predominant state for employment within the region.

Niche law schools

Niche law schools focus their resources on a particular field of law. They are not national law schools, although some are regional law schools. National law schools might have specialties as significant as those at niche schools, but they also have a breadth of curriculum that makes these specialties less important. Instead of trying to be the best general law school possible given limited resources, the niche schools have chosen an area of law in which they have some strength. To this they have added more faculty and more financial resources to gain more name recognition and to attract students interested in that subject area. Specialties have long included environmental law, intellectual property law, international law, and tax law. For example, Vermont Law School and Lewis & Clark Law School, both located in environmentally activist states, focus on environmental law.

There are numerous LL.M. programs in taxation; the schools that dominate tend to be national such as NYU or top state schools such as University of Florida. More recently, dispute resolution and healthcare law have become areas of focus, creating more niche schools.

Even if you have a strong interest that matches a niche school, I recommend you choose a national school if you have the opportunity, and seriously consider the niche school as a plausible backup. The reason for always choosing national over niche is that the niche schools typically have limited resources outside their niche. The rest of your legal education would suffer and, if you should change your interests, your decision to attend the school will not have been a good one. Even in the particular subject area you seek, a national school may be as strong or stronger.

Independent or stand-alone law schools

Fewer than twenty law schools have no university affiliation. They are known as independent or stand-alone law schools, and virtually all are nonprofit educational institutions. Some of these schools are stronger than some of the local law schools that are affiliated with universities, but virtually all of them fall into the bottom third or quarter of law schools.

A notable exception is Brooklyn Law School, which is widely considered to be among the top third of law schools. Its location in an attractive section of Brooklyn close to downtown Manhattan, its strong faculty, the quality of students it can attract, and its ability to place its top students at some of the most elite law firms in New York City, enable it to remain strong even without a formal university affiliation. Brooklyn offers joint program options with divisions of the City University of New York.

Other independent schools have worked out joint degree arrangements with universities in their local area, mitigating some of the disadvantages associated with the absence of university affiliation. At many of these independent law schools, you can acquire a very good legal education. At most of them, just as at the more locally oriented university affiliated law schools, there is more focus on the state bar exam than is the case at the national and regional law schools.

Unaccredited law schools

Unaccredited law schools are those which have not been approved or even provisionally approved by the American Bar Association, the national accrediting body for law schools. They are usually described as proprietary schools, indicating that they are for-profit educational institutions. Until 1995, the ABA had never granted accreditation to any school that was a for-profit institution although many, if not most, law schools had their origins as proprietary institutions. After an antitrust suit against the ABA in 1995, profit vs. nonprofit status is no longer a criterion the ABA can use in the decision whether to approve accreditation.

The reason that most of these schools do not achieve accreditation is that they devote fewer resources to hiring strong faculty members or to their libraries or other educational assets than is considered acceptable by the ABA. Most do not even try for accreditation because of the expense of meeting the standards set by the ABA.

Most unaccredited law schools are in California. Students from these schools are permitted to take the "Baby Bar" examination, formally known as the First Year Law Students Examination—FYLSE, after completing their first year of law school. Administered by the California State Bar Association to students from unaccredited law schools, the Baby Bar allows them to demonstrate that they have a foundation in certain first year subjects adequate to continue their education and take the General Bar Examination after graduation, just as those from accredited schools do. Although these students may one day be admitted to the Bar in California, they will not be able to practice in any other state.

Other states have provisions for graduates of unaccredited law schools in their states to qualify for the Bar in that state but, as is the case for California proprietary schools, typically there is no reciprocity with other states, restricting their graduates to practice in their home states. The faculty at these schools teach to the bar exam, hoping to effect a high passage rate. But, for example, in California, graduates of the unaccredited schools have a very low first-time-taker passage rate on the California Bar Exam, about 25 percent compared to 69 percent of graduates of ABA approved law schools.

These schools continue to exist because they can attract students who work full-time for whom distance from the accredited schools is a major drawback. They also admit students who have not been accepted at the accredited schools. (California is also one of very few states that still permit students to "read" law, studying under the supervision of an attorney or a judge for four years, and taking the Baby Bar, followed by the California bar years later.)

If you have the chance to attend an accredited law school, choose it over an unaccredited school even if the location is inconvenient and the cost significantly higher. Since employers want to hire from the best law schools possible, to maximize the chances that their new hires will expeditiously become members of the bar, and your goal is to secure legal employment, your investment in yourself is likely to pay off if you make that choice from the start.

DOES THE SIZE OF THE LAW SCHOOL MATTER?

In college, your graduating class might have been smaller than 100 students or larger than 10,000. You may have chosen a college based on the strength of a particular department; the invitation to attend an honors program, its business school, school of journalism, or some other specialized school within the college.

Although you may have heard that there are some very large law schools, the range in size in law schools is narrow by comparison with that among colleges. The largest law school has 622 full-time students and 10 part-time students in the first year class. The second largest law school entering class of full-time students is Harvard, with 550–560 in the entering class. Including part-time students, Georgetown has about 590 entering students, although only about 460 are full-time. Part-time students enter a four year program, so each student counts as three-fourths of a full-time student. There are only seven schools, three of which are public, with fewer than 100 full-time students and fewer than 5 part-time students in their entering classes. Most schools are in the range of 100–200 full-time students in an entering class. Of these, 46 are public schools and 52 are private. (All figures are taken from the LSAC web site.)

Because the larger schools typically divide their entering classes into smaller groups for the first-year courses, your experience with size will vary in a more complicated way than simply the size of the entering class. In its *Official Guide to Law Schools*, the LSAC web site provides information about the size of sections in the first year, the number of classes in the upper class curriculum with less than twenty-five people, and then in increments of twenty-five students up to one hundred plus. Data about the number of seminars and other small classes and about the number of clinical courses and fieldwork placements, where faculty contact is greater, is also available.

Economy of scale works for you at larger schools, which can actually provide more opportunities to do specialized work in a wide variety of subject areas in a more intimate environment than that existing in the basic courses.

But whatever the law school size, there are advantages and disadvantages. What is an advantage for one person may seem like a problem to another. For example, the advantage or disadvantage of the larger schools is that they do permit you to get lost in the crowd. You have to work harder to get the attention of faculty members and to get to know your fellow students. There is more competition to participate in some classes or some events than at smaller schools, although there are more classes and more events to choose from. On the upside, there are more faculty members to get to know, more fellow students from whom to choose friends who share your particular interests, and more student activities with different individuals participating. There is more of everything, including a larger alumni network. And more people get admitted.

The downside of the smaller school is fewer faculty members and fewer course offerings than at the larger schools. A small school is like any small community; everyone in the community knows just about everything about everyone else, a plus for some, a minus for others. If you have something embarrassing happen to you, everyone is likely to learn about it. If you have a relationship that doesn't work out, it can be harder because everyone else knows about it. Animosities can develop and everyone will know about them, in some cases taking sides.

On the upside, you get to know each other more quickly and more closely, and to feel that you belong. You are more likely to get to know the faculty with less effort on your part. If you are having trouble, people will know and will come to your aid. The smaller group can be cohesive and supportive, and feel more like a family. Graduates of the very small schools are typically intensely loyal.

Large, medium, and small law schools all work well, but which works best for you may be different from that which works best for your friends, your acquaintances, or even your twin sister. Where you gravitate is a very personal matter and is likely to be based on how best you learn and where you feel most comfortable. Visiting the schools will give you a feel, but your own past experience and instincts may be equally important indicators.

WHAT DOES STUDENT-TO-FACULTY RATIO CONSIST OF AND WHY SHOULD IT MATTER?

The student-to-faculty ratio is the number of students per faculty member. Theoretically, the lower the student-to-faculty ratio the more time each faculty member can spend with each student. A very high student-to-faculty ratio means that faculty members may be limited in the amount of time they can spend with each student. It does not always work out as a good predictor, since some faculty members shoulder a lot of the student mentoring, while others may have a great many outside commitments or comparatively little interest in individual students.

Some faculty members with a lot of outside commitments manage to spend a lot of time with students, while others who are always on campus guard their time to allow for more research and writing. For example, there are two well-known faculty members at HLS that you would expect would have little time to spend with students, Alan Dershowitz and Larry Tribe. Both actually spend a great deal of time with their students and are much more available than you would expect. They care deeply about their students and make them a high priority. When you are making choices, look deeper than the student-to-faculty ratio to assess the availability of faculty.

ATTRITION

Another consideration is attrition of the student body, or the degree to which your classmates are likely to be with you for the full extent of your legal education. Attrition is also one measure of the likelihood of graduating once you enter a law school. The level of attrition bears some relationship to the quality of school.

The total attrition from all law schools is about 10 percent. Some schools have a higher attrition rate, so that a smaller number graduate than begin law school. Schools at the top of the heap, which take a significant number of transfer students, may graduate more students than the number entering as first year students. The top schools have a nearly zero attrition rate. At the low end of schools, there may be as high as 32 percent attrition during or after the first year. There is additional attrition at the lower-ranked schools because of students transferring up the pecking order after the first year. Beyond that, some attrition is because of academic weakness or failure, but most is because students decide not to pursue the degree after they have started it. The latter is reassuring for those who are worried about their ability to succeed in law school, because it means that very few people fail out. Still, the fact that many decide to drop out is a clear indication that prelaw research and assessment are worth the time and effort.

FINAL THOUGHTS

The "big picture" overview of law schools provided in this chapter is meant to provide some of the basic things to think about as you begin your exploration of where you might want to attend. Knowing what law schools are like and some of the differences among them will help you make informed choices, choices best matched to your needs and interests.

Before we get to the issue of matching you with schools, another piece of the law school picture is why and how law schools are ranked and whether rankings should be of concern to you as you think about where you want to apply.

CHAPTER SIX

Ranking the Law Schools

RANKING EDUCATIONAL INSTITUTIONS HAS become big business in the last two decades. To its supporters, ranking schools is an important service to consumers, including prospective students and prospective employers. To its detractors, ranking uses flawed methodology—which is subject to politics or manipulation—to sell magazines or books, and it has a corrosive influence on the educational mission of those institutions it ranks.

The most widely known, used, and abused ranking system is that produced by *U.S. News & World Report*. *U.S. News* is not in the education business; it is in the news business, informing the public on what they consider it has a right to know. It is also in the business of selling magazines. It is a natural consequence that *U.S. News* would respond to the interest of the consumer (you the applicant, and others who want some basis for comparing law schools) by trying to make some sense out of complex and sometimes confusing information. What is important for you to understand, to help you make your own ranking from an informed perspective, is what they do successfully and what they fail to do.

To develop its ranking system, *U.S. News* picked a number of factors, some survey driven and some with a statistical basis, and developed a methodology for quantifying and cumulating them to produce an ordered ranking.

To inform yourself about how rankings are determined and what factors are weighed, look at the *U.S. News* web site (usnews.com/sections/rankings) and click on "law schools," where you will find an explanation of the methodology used. You can also go to leiterrankings.com to see a critique of the *U.S. News* ranking system and an alternative ranking system by Prof. Brian Leiter of the University of Texas Law School. Leiter evaluates and ranks faculty scholarship, student quality, and job placement in law teaching, Supreme Court clerkships, and elite law firms. Leiter's system has its own flaws which, to his credit, he acknowledges.

Educational institutions do not want to be ranked, particularly by organizations like the media from outside of the educational framework. They legitimately say that the factors under scrutiny are too complex to be reduced to a single number or aggregation of numbers. Their contention is that to do so is irresponsible and educationally unsound. The deans of the ABA-accredited law schools have written a letter denouncing ranking systems for law schools and encouraging applicants to think for themselves in choosing a law school. They are right to do so, but even with the letter denouncing ranking of law schools, the schools themselves are not innocent bystanders. Because of pressures on the educational institutions, in our case the law schools, there is a tendency for those who have been ranked higher than their peer schools to call attention to that fact and to use the rankings for competitive advantage. And so begins the vicious cycle of schools denouncing and touting the rankings. The media and the schools thus form a curious partnership that both inform and confuse you.

WHAT IS WRONG WITH THE RANKINGS?

There are methodological problems with quantifying data that are subject to impression and opinion, although opinion surveys can be helpful considered on their own. Those data not subject to impression can be manipulated by the schools. The combination of the two can be misleading to those who rely on rankings to help them make decisions. The schools are complicit in this, both by manipulation of the data and by how they treat quantifiable data on your application.

U.S. News sends one set of questionnaires to deans and faculty members at law schools around the country. They send another set to lawyers and judges. According to U.S. News' description of their own methodology, 71 percent of deans and faculty answer a questionnaire about the quality of fellow law schools, whereas only 29 percent of lawyers and judges do. Deans and faculty have good reason to respond, if only to report well on their own schools as compared to the competition. The lawyers and judges have less reason to respond, and fewer do. Of the lawyers, most are at elite law firms, and thus were more likely to attend top schools. This is also true of judges. The likelihood is that they will give their own law schools top ratings, and this favors the top schools, although it may not make distinctions among them.

Having said that, the rankings do a reasonable job of roughly describing where a law school falls in the relationship to other law schools. The key is to understand them as approximate rather than as precise indicators; and to recognize how they can be manipulated.

HOW CAN SCHOOLS MANIPULATE THE RANKINGS?

With respect to admissions selectivity, which accounts for 25% of their rank, law schools can manipulate rankings in three ways: the LSAT, the GPA, and the admission rate.

To maximize the median LSAT score and median GPA of its entering class, those selecting the student body can focus on small differences in these quantitative data when making admissions decisions. One point on the LSAT can make the difference if the school is focused on reporting a higher LSAT average. In evaluating GPA, misuse of the numbers can result in a preference toward a student who has attended a college where grades have been inflated, or one where the student body is weaker and higher grades mean less, or toward a less rigorous set of courses over a set that are tougher, simply in order to report a higher median.

Some schools use techniques like admitting smaller classes in the first year and increasing the number of transfer applicants, whose LSAT and GPA are not part of the medians, to make up the difference in enrollment.

To boost the admission rate, schools can and do invite large numbers of applicants to apply without paying the application fee, in order to improve the acceptance rate. There are valid reasons to do this if there is a realistic chance for admission, but the grapevine suggests the decision to do so is frequently driven by the rankings. There is a limit to the amount of manipulation possible because a critical part of the decision of who will attend remains with the admitted applicants, but what is done can be enough to give the law school an edge against a particular rival.

Placement success accounts for 20% of the rank, with 18% related to employment and 2% related to bar exam success. Schools have been known to manipulate this data by hiring any unemployed graduate to work for the school, and by counting any employment as relevant. Since employment need not be in the legal profession itself, many nonprofessional jobs count as employment.

With respect to faculty resources, which accounts for 15% of the rank, schools can allocate as many dollars as possible to "expenditures on behalf of students."

With respect to specializations, be especially wary. Faculty members with a special interest in these specializations are invited to nominate up to fifteen schools in each field. This can lead to political "gaming" of the system, with heavy participation rates from schools with a vested interest in being included on the list.

WHY DO RANKINGS MATTER?

Rankings matter because many groups care about how they come out. Applicants care because they think rankings help them make initial and sometimes final choices of the best schools to attend. Employers care because rankings help them decide where to go to recruit the better students. Students care because employers care, and the job market is their next focus after law school. The rankings confirm whether or not their school is valued for what they think it is, and the ranking reflects on them as a group. Alumni care because employers care and because rankings can add or subtract value to or from their degrees. Presidents and deans care because alumni, employers, students, and applicants care. Admissions and Career Services Deans care because rankings can affect how easy or difficult their jobs will be that next year and even whether they will keep those jobs.

CAN RANKINGS ACTUALLY BE HELPFUL TO YOU?

Rankings can be especially helpful when you are trying to narrow the field of where you will apply. At this stage, you are making broader choices and the difference in the rankings between schools X and Y is not determinative. You may well apply to both. You may be able to check general rankings to evaluate schools in which you have some interest or where you have determined that you are a possible or likely candidate for admission.

Added to all the other information you have been looking at, rankings can help with a ballpark evaluation. When you get to the stage of choosing among offers of admission, and you begin to split hairs, using the rankings for other than a broad perspective could result in your making a choice that will not serve you as well as would another reason for choosing a particular school.

One of the best ways to use the rankings is to create your own system, using the factors that are of the most importance to you. Use the research that other ranking systems have done, and add anything else that is of interest to you about which you can gather data from the ABA pages in the *Official Guide*. By doing this, you may begin to understand just how inaccurate and arbitrary the ranking systems in existence can be, but you can also learn what factors matter to you as you make your own choices.

Rankings are here to stay. They are flawed, but they can be of some help to you if you keep them in perspective, understanding the potential flaws in how they measure, and deciding which measurements are important to you.

CHAPTER SEVEN

Deciding Where to Apply

A SSUMING YOU HAVE DONE the research described in the chapter on deciding whether to apply to law school, you are now ready to choose the law schools to which you want to apply. Narrowing the choices of law schools may be easier than narrowing the choices for applying to college, but it still takes some effort on your part.

First and foremost is the very practical consideration of where you can get in. After determining a range of schools where you are a "likely," "possible," or "long-shot" candidate for admission, you can match your interests and abilities with the offerings at the schools in your range.

PROBABILITY OF ADMISSION

Considering your probability of admission at particular schools is an important reality check for you. The practical matter of finding your range for probability of admission involves matching your grades and scores with the grids shown in the *Official Guide to Law Schools* on the LSAC web site (http://officialguide.lsac.org/). Go to the searchable edition and click on "LSAC Data Search" (search for schools based on UGPA and LSAT score). Enter your undergraduate grades and LSAT score, choose "likelihood" and "ascending order" as search criteria. Note that there are some schools that have elected not to participate in this search tool; you can see which ones by clicking on "nonparticipating schools" at the top of the screen where the other schools are listed.

There are some anomalies in terms of likelihood. You can make a judgment about the anomalies by looking at the "bands" for UGPA and LSAT individually. A few schools where the likelihood is very high are mixed in with the schools where the likelihood is predictably low. The screen will show the name of the law school and a chart that shows your grades and scores, with your scoreband, against a band between 25th and 75th percentiles on the grades and scores. It also provides a range of likelihood for a person with your numerical credentials.

There are two other places to check how you match against a particular school. The first is the Law School Description for the school. Some schools will include a grid showing the recent experience of applicants within ranges of grades plotted against ranges of scores. Other schools have a short explanation of why the grid is not included. Looking at the grids and estimating where your credentials fall within the grid can help you pinpoint your probability. If you are close to the edge of another box for either grades or scores, check that too to refine your estimate of your probabilities.

The second is in the ABA Law School Data, where there is a listing of the percentiles of grades and scores for the most recent entering class. If you find that you are above the 75th percentile on both criteria for a given school, your chances are very high. If you are below the 25th percentile on both, the chances of admission are very slim. If you are above the 75th on one and below the 25th on the other, you have what is called "discrepant predictors," and your chances will depend heavily on the documentation you provide that bolsters the higher percentile and mitigates the lower one. It also depends, as do your chances in every scenario, on factors like your recommendations and experience.

Let us consider an example of how to use these probability tools. If your grades are 3.67 and your score is 169, your search results will show Harvard with a likelihood of less than 25 percent, Berkeley and Penn in the middle between 25 and 50 percent, Michigan and NYU just under 50 percent, and Duke, Virginia, and Georgetown straddling the 50 percent likelihood. Harvard is a very long-shot, Berkeley and Penn are long-shots, Michigan and NYU are the low end of possible, while Duke, Virginia, and Georgetown are in your range of possible. If you are from California, Michigan, or Virginia, you can raise your probabilities for your home state public school, based on your in-state status. If you are not from those states, your probabilities for these schools will be lower than it appears. Your range of likely schools includes BC, Vanderbilt, Fordham, and USC among the private schools, and if you are from California, Illinois, Texas, Virginia (for William and Mary), or Washington, you have an even higher likelihood of admission to your home state school.

Some of the schools also show a grid as part of their law school description. When you look at Duke, the box in which your credentials fall is for 3.50–3.75 and 165–169. It shows that 134 of 491, or about 1 out of 4 applicants were admitted. You are right in the middle for GPA, but close to the top for LSAT. So check the box for 170–175. The chances rise to 156/225, or about 2 out of 3. You would fall at the high end of the first group and the low end of the second. When you check the ABA statistics for GPA and LSAT, you are at the 75th percentile, just above the median on the LSAT, but just above the 25th percentile on the GPA.

For more detail or for schools that do not show up on your screen, you can check the ABA information for the individual school at the same site for some gross estimates. Every school is required to publish the 25th and 75th percentiles and the medians for both UGPA and LSAT. If your grades and scores fall between the 25th and 75th percentiles it is worth applying. If you have reason to believe, for reasons of background, experience, race or ethnicity, expertise, or any other reason that you are likely to be of special interest to that school, remember that 25 percent of the admitted class falls below the 25th percentile on one of those criteria or the other, although probably not both. Look at the grids; if anyone is admitted with credentials like yours, it may be worth a long-shot application.

Read the chapters on quantifiable factors and qualitative factors as you consider your likelihood of admission. They will help you modulate your probabilities and maximize your choices within the range of possibility. Here you can factor in the quality of your undergraduate school, the rigor of your course selection, and the extent to which grades are inflated or not, to refine your probabilities.

At top schools like Harvard and NYU, the average applicant applies to at least nine law schools. Let us assume that you will follow this pattern, more or less. Choose at least two schools where you have a better than 75 percent chance of being admitted (likely), at least three schools where your chances are about 25–75 percent (possible), and no more than two schools where your chances are less than 25 percent (long-shot). This gives you a bit of wiggle room to choose some additional schools taking into account your own reasons for adjusting probability or for some of the reasons outlined below.

Once you have determined the range of likely, possible, or long-shot, you are ready for other considerations. Most of your attention here should be on choosing likely or possible schools.

HOW DO I DISTINGUISH BETWEEN LAW SCHOOLS?

How do you choose which law school you want to attend? Starting again at the LSAC web site, you can access copious and fairly standard information about all of the close to two hundred ABA-accredited law schools, including a four-page spread on each school. Two of the pages are provided by the school as the Law School Description in text they choose, although certain sections are strongly urged by the LSAC. The other two pages include quantitative data required by the LSAC and ABA as full disclosure of important "consumer" information for applicants. You can slice and dice the available information in a variety of ways.

You can also get to the web sites of all the individual ABA-accredited law schools through this site, to explore those schools you have identified as of interest to you. You can begin to research schools based on criteria important to you. The hard part is deciding what is important to you and not getting caught up in minutia that don't matter very much in your case. The information available can be overwhelming, and sometimes misleading, and figuring out what matters can be complicated. Still, if such factors as location, size of class, or availability of merit scholarships and the like are critical to your decision, you can begin to narrow the list of schools you want to explore more fully.

Location

One large category to consider is location, location, location. Just as in buying real estate, location may be an important consideration for narrowing the choice of schools to which to apply. The searchable edition of the *Official Guide* lets you search on locations according to state or geographic region. Some of the issues related to location follow.

First, where do you want to spend the next three years? Do you want to be in an urban or rural setting? Is being on a traditional campus important to you or would you be happier at a school whose campus is woven into the fabric of the city?

Second, where are you hoping to work after you graduate? Except for the graduates of the top national schools, most lawyers end up practicing in the locality or region in which they attend law school.

Third, if you have no geographic preference, consider schools in or near large metropolitan areas that have large law firms. After hiring new associates from the top national schools, these firms typically hire the top graduates from the local law schools in or near their cities. The same consideration holds for the possibility of finding law-related part-time work while you are in school. (The Leiter ranking web site provides a demonstration of this.)

Cost

Cost is an important factor in choosing where to attend law school, but premature to consider at this stage. Understanding the cost of your legal education is complicated by financial aid, including both need-based aid and merit scholarships, neither of which you can know before being admitted. The only cost factor to consider at this point is whether to apply to your state law school, if your state has one or more. In general, if the school is within your range of probability, it makes sense to include it, regardless of tuition and living costs.

Special programs

If you have ideas about specific programs or specializations you want in a prospective law school, look for law schools that offer them. You might be able to locate schools that share your interests by an initial search on the *Official Guide* searchable edition, but you may find too many schools responding to the key words you enter. Alternatively, you can begin by looking at what law schools offer in their specializations, letting that stimulate your thinking about how your background and interests relate to what the schools have to offer.

By alternating between your interests and what schools offer, you can learn about individual schools while refining your own interests and goals. You might identify schools where your interests and background give you an edge. Remember also that part of this exercise is to identify features of a school that match your experience or expertise and thus might make you more attractive to them. By going through this process, you might be in a position to call attention to the potential match in your application. You might even turn a long-shot school into a possible one.

If after some exploration you find that location, size, or specializations don't matter to you, as they don't to a great many applicants, there may be other facets that are important to you beyond these, including affiliation with a particular university, type of school, joint programs, the diversity of the student body, or the reputation of the faculty. If so, let those factors help you winnow down the number of schools to which you apply.

Remember that you are just choosing possibilities here; you are not making your final choice. Keep an open mind for new considerations and ideas. Don't obsess too much on the details until after you have been admitted and must make choices with real options in mind. The more investigation you do now, the less you will have to do later, but later you can focus on your top handful of options.

THE FIVE R'S: READING, RESEARCH, REPU- TATION, RECONNAISSANCE, AND REVIEW

The five R's represent the different ways you can undertake in-depth exploration of the law schools that have made it through your own initial screens, including those described previously. As you begin your explorations, here are some important steps to take, in whatever order works best for you. I have ordered them by relative ease of implementation:

1. **Read** about the schools in printed materials, on the Internet, and in news articles (which might be found on the Internet).

2. **Research** what interests you both at the schools and in general. Find out all you can about whatever piques your interest, and see what the schools say about it.

3. **Reputation:** learn about schools from how they are perceived by others. Ask friends, relatives, lawyers, and judges what they know about the schools you are considering. Talk to students at the school and students at rival schools. Get as many perspectives as possible. At law forums and fairs, talking to school representatives can make this very efficient.

4. **Reconnaissance:** visit and see for yourself.

5. **Review** and refine your goals and assets on a regular basis as you consider where you would like to be. Do this on a continuing basis from the applicant stage onward.

Let's take a close look at each of these steps.

Reading

There is some easily accessible reading information on the LSAC web site. When you were deciding whether to apply, you were looking at legal education generally. Now you want to follow the links to specific schools.

Read their materials to see what they emphasize. How does it fit with what you want? And with what else you know about them? Look behind the marketing materials. Do they really have something different from what is available at schools with whom they are in competition for the same applicants?

For example, if you have a science background and have worked summers in government or nonprofit organizations concerned with the environment, look for schools that highlight environmental law, and then consider all the things you have done that will promote their interest in you. Also consider how big the field is that they are promoting. Are there a significant number of people being employed in that field each year? Is it one of the specialties in demand in the legal profession?

Research

You can research the individual schools on their web sites, using the link from the LSAC web site. Delving into the process in more depth can be a helpful spur. Continue your research efficiently at one of the LSAC forums or a law fair at or near your school. Some applicants from remote places travel to the nearest forum, spending the weekend and having in-depth conversations with officers from all the schools in which they are interested. Because this is a time that the admissions deans have devoted specifically to reach out to applicants and to explain their schools, including how the admissions process works, etc., you may find that this is your best opportunity to meet with them.

Having done your research on the web sites, you can be equipped with questions that you can explore with representatives of many law schools. The more you know, the better your questions will be, and the more you will learn from the panels and the representatives you meet at their individual tables. I can assure you, from my own experience, that the Deans of Admissions, admissions officers, students, and alumni on the other side of the table will be delighted to talk with you at length if you have done your homework before attending. You will also learn much more from them if you have done some preparatory background work on their schools. The admissions officer may even remember meeting with you when he or she sees your application.

You will find that, especially for those deans from the elite schools, it is extremely difficult to meet with them when you visit their schools as an applicant. The tables turn again once you are admitted, when you will find them much more available. This is simply triage, law school admissions style. If the Dean of

Admissions were available to all applicants, he or she would find that there was no time for anything else but meeting with would-be students. At the forums, those in attendance want nothing more than to talk with you, and the more you have done your research, the more you and they will enjoy the interaction.

The forums are very helpful but they are not perfect. At some of the busier ones, you may find it hard to get near the person you most want to meet, because of the crowd around the table. This will be especially true at the top national schools and at all the local schools and even the regional schools for the forum host city. You may have to wait your chance. I recommend that you arrive early in the morning, leave or attend the workshops during the most crowded time, and return toward the end of the day. Many of the forums are two-day events, so you will have four opportunities to hit the least busy times.

You can also hover at the table of the school you are interested in and listen to the questions from other attendees and the answers they get. Take note of questions and answers that interest you and use your time with the representative to follow up or to delve deeper. You can also learn a lot from hearing the conversations that develop in the give-and-take between the admissions representatives and other prospective students.

The busier schools at these events will likely have admissions officers, students, and alumni in attendance. Talking with any one of these, or to each, will reveal a more complete picture of the school.

Reputation

Reputation refers both to the relative prestige of the law school and how students, faculty, alumni, and employers regard the school, its faculty, and its graduates, including that of the university with which it is affiliated. If you have any notion of cross-registration or of applying for a joint program, the offerings at the university are important.

Talk to your prelaw adviser again, this time with specific schools on the agenda. Each year, the person designated as prelaw adviser at your college receives a Prelaw Adviser Action Report from LSAC, indicating which applicants from that school were admitted to which law schools. Often, they are willing to share the report with the next crop of applicants. The report includes the academic and demographic indicators (GPA, LSAT, major, and year of graduation) for the applicants included, although the applicants are not identified. By matching your information with that on the report, you can get a general sense of your chances of being admitted.

Remember that your prelaw adviser may advise you against applying to some schools that might be a reach for you. Their success is measured partly by whether students get into schools to which they apply, and they will try to direct you to schools where you are likely to get in. Long-shots have a way of being improbable and prelaw advisers don't thrive on large numbers of disappointed students. They are likely to be cautious in their encouragement.

Ask people in the profession. They have hired graduates in the past. Or they may be a recent grad from the school in which you are interested. If you are interested in clerking for a judge after finishing law school, find out how many graduates clerk and where do they clerk—at the federal, state, or local level? Ask people working for organizations you would like to work for. You may be making contact with a future employer. But do your homework first, so that you don't look like a dilettante, or just generally unprepared. Seeming clueless won't serve you well if you hope to get a job with the organization someday.

Reconnaissance (visit)
As you did while deciding whether to apply, visit a school of interest virtually before you go in person. This visit is focused

on whether you want to apply. During your "virtual visit" you can also plan your physical excursion so that you can maximize the experience. For example, you might learn about upcoming speakers and events open to the public that you can time your visit to include. Some schools hold online chat rooms or information sessions. Chat rooms are a lot like virtual visits, where the school has arranged for people who can field your questions on almost any law school–related topic to be available at a particular time. These also can be helpful for seeing what kinds of questions are on other applicants' minds and how they are answered by the school, and are most relevant if you are seriously considering applying to the school hosting the event.

A physical visit will yield much more of a feel for the institution than will a virtual one. One of the negative side effects of being able to visit law schools "virtually" is that many prospective law students don't take advantage of opportunities to interact and talk directly in person with living, breathing law school admissions officers.

You may not be able to visit all the law schools to which you apply before you apply, but try to visit the most accessible, to get a sense of what might be important to you. Then research those factors online or in whatever literature you can get your hands on, to see how others, to which you might apply, stack up in comparison.

If at all possible, visit while school is in session, preferably not during exams unless you want to see how panicky people become. Try your best to equalize the conditions under which you visit each school.

If you are still in college or in a location that has a law school nearby, you might find that your interest will be piqued first by attending a law school class. Most law schools provide this opportunity for prospective applicants. Call the school or schools near you to see about visiting a class. The admissions office is usually a good place to start. They are the most likely office to have an interest in your seeing their law school first-hand. While you're at it, see if they hold information sessions for interested applicants, and whether they include tours of the school for applicants. Many law schools do and some even host open houses for interested applicants. Whatever they offer, take advantage of the opportunity for any event directed at applicants, even if it is not at a school you hope to attend. You will learn something regardless and you might even change your mind about the school itself.

But don't stop there. Take note in your virtual visit when there are speakers or events coming up at the law school. Many law schools, particularly those at the top of the pecking order, have speakers and events on a regular basis where their students can hear from those in practice, the judiciary, government, and legal education. Many schools have distinguished speaker series, and some of the distinguished speakers may be professors at other law schools. Typically, these speeches or events are open to the entire academic community, and some are open to the general public.

The top schools may have competing events on the same day. It could be a full-time job for students to take advantage of what they have to offer. For this reason, some events are less well attended than you might expect, and you might have a chance not only to attend, but also to participate actively and speak to the presenter after the event. Familiarize yourself with what goes on at the school or schools near you; take advantage of as many as you can that interest you. This can be a wonderful way to get a feel for the life of the law school and for what lawyers are concerned about. It can be a valuable resource for all college students, throughout their academic careers. What you learn outside the classroom, but within the academic environment, can help your law school application, your legal education, and your legal career.

Review

Continually assess what you think as you take each of the other steps. Reviewing what you have learned and checking in with yourself periodically during the application process is only the beginning. Do it without obsessing on the final answer, but as a continuous comfort-seeking exercise. Keep long-term goals in mind. Do you want to go for the "big time"? Or are you strictly locally oriented and happy with the idea of being a small town lawyer. Are your aspirations too modest or do they feel just right? Keeping your options flexible may mean aiming high in your applications.

HOW DO YOU TELL SUBSTANCE FROM MARKETING?

Getting past the marketing hype from the schools can be a challenge. Once you have signed up for the LSAT, you may be bombarded by direct mail promotional materials from law schools, just as you were when you applied to college. This comes to you courtesy of the Candidate Referral Service described above. They might be writing to you because the information they have on you suggests you would be a strong candidate, or they might just want to expand their applicant pool.

Learning how to distinguish marketing from substance will take work and a critical look at claims made by the school. Glitzy publications often hide lack of substance. These glossy publications created by the law schools also tend to make them all look alike. Some schools have started blogs that are marketing in disguise, a gimmick to get you to read about something that they are trying to highlight. Look behind the glitz and into the substance of the blog to see what if anything is really there, or if it is just another way to market a program that is not different from those at other schools.

Decide whether what is there is really important and valuable to you personally and to your professional training. For example, if School X is promoting a program in international law, how many courses do they offer in the subject, and are those courses offered every year, or even every other year? Do they cover both public and private international law? Do they cover the whole world and, if not, which parts? Are there clinical courses in the subject area? How many faculty members teach in the subject area, and do they also teach other subjects as well? Have the faculty members published articles or books in international law? Some "programs in international law" are merely an aggregation of courses on the subject, as opposed to having a number of research programs, institutes, speaker series, etc., with a faculty member or group of faculty members or even an administrator coordinating the activities. Ask yourself how the school you are researching stacks up in this respect.

MERIT SCHOLARSHIPS

Another marketing tool is the lure of a merit scholarship. Ask yourself whether the merit scholarship program you might apply for is simple discounted tuition or if it includes a meaningful academic component.

To make ends meet, schools offering large amounts of merit scholarship money must raise the money somewhere. Most of that money comes from raising tuition, so that some students pay for the privilege of attending school with those who win the scholarship. If you are applying to School X because its merit scholarship program includes half the class or more, you may just be applying for a discount of tuition at that school. The school is betting that you will be in the top half of the class when you graduate, but if you are not, you could lose big on the salary front when you graduate as compared to graduating from a stronger school.

Compare the average salary for graduates of this school with School Y that has few if any merit scholarships. If there is no difference, you have little to lose. If the average salary is higher at School Y, consider whether the merit scholarship is worth the risk. If the merit scholarship school is one you want to attend anyway, go for it! If not, you may be better off saving the application fee.

FINAL THOUGHTS

As you research you schools of interest, following the five R's, keep these caveats in mind as you make your choices:

- Don't apply to any school you would be unwilling to attend if it is your only offer.
- Don't get sucked in by marketing.
- Keep an open mind.

CHAPTER EIGHT

Behind the Scenes in the Admissions Office and the Admissions Committee

UNLESS YOU HAVE ACTUALLY worked in an admissions office for a law school or some other graduate or professional school, what happens in the law school admissions office and committee can seem like a complete mystery to you. Applicants frequently waste time and mental energy trying to figure out what goes on in the minds of those who make the admissions selection decisions. "What do I need to do or have to get in?" may be foremost in your mind. Subsets of these questions are "how do you weigh the LSAT? letters of recommendation? the GPA?" and so on down the list of criteria that are included in the selection process. "What is your school looking for?" with the subtext "how do I make myself look like that?" is a common query.

You may think that if you can find out what decision makers think is important, you can shape your application to get you that offer of admission. If you are in the early stages of applying and concerned about your chances of admission, time and energy spent on trying to psyche out the minds of those on the admissions committee could be to the detriment of pondering the more significant question of whether you actually want to attend law school and which school is the best match for your interests and abilities.

One of the most important reasons not to try to psyche out the admissions committee is that you can come up with the wrong answers. This is evidenced by some of the misinformation that is passed among applicants in some of the threaded discussions on law school admissions web sites. Another is that even within a given admissions committee there is likely to be a difference of opinion with respect to individual applicants or about what factors are most important. Even within the microcosm of those faculty members with whom I worked, I found that some focused heavily on writing ability while others cared more about strong quantitative skills. At Harvard, it took a number of people to decide to admit an applicant, so a whole variety of factors and a number of perspectives weighed into each individual decision.

The best way to approach the process is to be true to yourself. If you have answered the question of whether you actually want to go to law school, know yourself and your abilities, and have given thought to which schools best match your interests and abilities, you will make the best case for yourself.

The questions below are sometimes asked directly by applicants, and sometimes I have been told by admitted students that they wish they had known to ask them. By answering them, I aim to make the admissions selection process transparent and give you a peek behind the scenes at the admissions office. Although admissions offices and admissions committees vary widely, much of what I will have to say is common to most.

FREQUENTLY ASKED QUESTIONS

Why do some schools contact me when I have not expressed any interest in them?

Once you have taken the LSAT, if you checked the box permitting law schools to contact you (and the vast majority of candidates do), you may be identified by a search through the

Candidate Referral Service of the Law School Admissions Council, as described above under CRS. There is a good chance that you will receive unsolicited publication materials from schools, and you may be contacted by email as well. You may be invited to apply, to visit the school at an open house, to meet with a representative of the school at a forum or law fair or when the representative visits your school, and/or to attend a panel discussion at which someone from the school is a participant.

Schools typically devote most of the fall to outreach and to meeting personally with prospective applicants. One goal is to generate as many applications as possible; another is to present a strong personalized image of their schools.

The invitation to apply may suggest that you have a good chance of being admitted to that school, or it may simply mean that you are within the range of possibility for admission and the school wants to maximize the number of applications from which it can choose the entering class (see the chapter on rankings).

To understand how decisions are made, we look first at the decision makers, the variety of models of selection, and how they work. Different models for selection vary with respect to both the kinds of people involved and the priorities set by the decision makers.

Who makes the decision on my application?

Who are the decision makers? When you applied to college, they were predominantly professional admissions officers. For law school, they are admissions administrators, faculty members, sometimes students, and rarely alumni. At some schools, all admissions decisions are made by faculty members of the admissions committee. At others, all are made by the top admissions administrator. Most schools are somewhere in the middle, with a cooperative effort by faculty members and administrators. Some of these schools also have input by students, either as full fledged voting members of the committee or as a subcommittee, making

making recommendations to the decision makers. At schools with very large applicant pools, administrators play a major role simply because faculty members have limited time to devote to the effort, and the sheer number of applications that must be sifted through. You should be prepared for the possibility that any combination of these groups of people will be judging what you have done and what you say about it. In effect, you should think of all of these as your judges.

What do the various members of the admissions committee contribute to the decision?

Admissions administrators serve as the repository of information about the undergraduate schools, including the quality of each school, the rigor of particular majors or individual courses at different undergrad schools, and even the language used by frequent recommenders from the larger "feeder" schools. There are applicants from too many schools for the whole committee to be fully knowledgeable. For example, at HLS there are applicants from more than 900 undergraduate schools each year. At any given time, the student body includes representatives from between 250 and 275 undergraduate institutions.

Approximately twenty-five institutions typically send a contingent of ten or more students each year. These are the "big feeder" schools. Invariably, Harvard College has been the largest feeder school for Harvard Law School, with 325–425 applicants each year. The pattern is replicated in most college/graduate school relationships within universities and is typical of the top law schools. Virtually every applicant applies to the law school affiliated with his or her own undergraduate school.

Because so many apply from Harvard College, the admissions committee at HLS knows more about Harvard courses and transcripts than about any other school. Much is also known about another forty or fifty colleges and universities from which several students came to HLS each year.

Every law school has its top feeder schools, about which it has detailed information. If you graduated from a school outside the top feeder group at some of the schools to which you are applying, you would be well advised to gather documentation from recommenders and other official sources at your school about the degree of difficulty of individual courses and overall academic programs.

Outside the curriculum, administrators can tell faculty members tidbits about which extracurricular activities at given undergraduate schools are substantial and which constitute puffery. For example, the position of student body president varies in importance with respect both to competition for the position and to its role in the life of the school. Its impact on school governance can also vary over time. When the student body president plays a major role in school governance, or routinely deals with important issues, the incumbent can develop strong leadership, teamwork, negotiation, and decision making skills. At the other end of the scale is a role helping to plan routine events and rubber stamping administration decisions, with no real skills development. The degree to which holding the position may affect the admissions decision for the incumbent reflects the development of skills rather than holding of the title.

Administrators can also tell the committee if the personal statement resembles those in the books that purport to have been "successful" at getting the writers admitted, or a lot like others received by the school. As readers of all the applications, the admissions staff can see and note "trends" in what applicants are focused on, and can identify suspicious coincidences between applications.

Faculty committee members bring their own experience in teaching and working with past students to consideration of the files they read. From that experience, they develop opinions about undergraduate academic preparation, and about which outside activities are relevant for the study of law; for example, debate competitions, meaningful leadership positions, teamwork experience, and community involvement. Student members can comment on courses and undergraduate extracurricular activities at their own undergraduate schools. They have access to scuttlebutt from their fellow students about colleges other than their own. Being from the same generation as most applicants, they have insight into hot topics, as well as into exaggeration in applications. They help the rest of the committee understand the applicant mind-set. Those from minority groups educate their fellow committee members about the special pressures and obstacles their particular minority group members face.

Alumni members, in the rare cases that they serve on the admissions committee, bring their individual perspectives as members of the profession, potential employers, and former students at the law school.

How are admissions decisions made?

One difference between admissions offices at law schools and those at colleges is the size of the staff and committee. Colleges devote many more resources to admissions than do law schools. There is hand holding during the college admissions process; most candidates are interviewed either by admissions officers or by alumni interviewers. There are virtually no interviews by law school admissions offices, other than for those on the waitlist (a few exceptions include Northwestern) and any hand holding is done by lower level staff when you call or email the school with your worries.

Because of the limited resources devoted to admissions at law schools, efficiency is key. At the larger schools, when the process is a collaboration between administrators and faculty, the procedures are designed to get through the applications expeditiously. Instead of having the whole committee read large numbers of applications, followed by meetings to discuss them, the applications are allocated and circulated according to probability of admission.

To chart the likely path of your application at given schools, examine the profile grids offered in the *Official Guide to Law Schools* published by the LSAC and ABA. The top applications, those with a 75+ percent chance of being admitted, are typically read initially by the Dean or Director of Admissions, and then sent on to faculty members of the committee with comments and a recommendation on a vote to admit or hold for further consideration. Those with a 50 percent or lower chance of admission are typically read by readers specifically hired and trained in what to look for in applications. Those in the middle are read by admissions officers, who possess experienced judgment about what constitutes a competitive applicant.

Each group of readers chooses the best of their candidates, typically 10–20 percent, to pass up the line. As these applications are compared with those read initially at the next level, some are winnowed out and some are handed up the line, with approximately 10 percent of the lower groups making it to the faculty members of the committee to be compared to the high probability applicants. During my time at HLS, typically 1,500–2,000+ applications out of 6,000–8,000 would make it through the gauntlet to be voted on by the Dean of Admissions and the faculty members of the Committee. Of these, about 800–825 would be offered admission for the 550–560 places in the class.

Shaping the class of students with strong accomplishments and varied interests, talents, and backgrounds in order to enhance the educational experience for all is an important objective. To accomplish that objective, many applications must be compared with one another. Because the stakes are high for the class at HLS, where two out of three admitted applicants will be in the class, there is more reason for faculty members to carefully scrutinize potential candidates and to comb through a large group of highly accomplished applicants to build the class.

At the other end of the spectrum is the strictly administrative model, used by a number of schools with large applicant pools, where the Dean of Admissions chooses the entire class. A very efficient model, it also uses readers and other staff members to read the low end of the pool, and bump up those applications that look stronger than their numbers. This model has the advantage of one person's overview, having considered all the most competitive applications, in shaping the class to the extent possible. The impact of each admissions offer is less because typically only one out of three or more admitted applicants will accept the offer. Shaping the class typically results from admitting applicants from the wait-list.

The disadvantage of this model is that it lacks the perspective of several people looking at the same application with the possibility of one person becoming a strong advocate. An experienced admissions dean can sometimes look at candidates with a view toward satisfying others' perspectives, but that can be an iffy proposition.

Many schools have adopted a process that combines the administrative model with some moderate faculty input. The admissions dean is charged with denying the bottom of the pool, admitting the top, and sending to the faculty members a small number of borderline cases, in what my colleague Richard Badger from University of Chicago likes to call the "zone of serious consideration." The size of the group can vary, but includes enough to admit the rest of the class and create a wait-list for any additional slots that open in the summer before school starts. The faculty members have a lot less to read in this scenario, and devote less time to it, but the cases they consider are close ones, and therefore important.

At schools where the applicant pool is small and there is concern about filling the class with students who can do the work and complete the program, faculty members might be heavily involved. Careful scrutiny is needed to find and evaluate qualities that might enable otherwise shaky candidates to succeed.

With so many applications to the top schools, how can they possibly read and give a fair chance to each of them?

The top schools have more flexibility than others in selecting applicants they think will enhance the experience of other students at the school and have more interest in making those selections.

By circulating applications as described above, those filed well before the deadline can be read by all appropriate readers within a reasonable time after the materials in them can be gathered. Funneling the strongest applications to the decision makers from initial readers allows each application to receive full consideration. In my experience at HLS, at least two people read each application, to reduce the possibility that one person's perspective could eliminate a candidate from consideration. Careful reading of each application is the only way to assure finding a diamond in the rough. The key to success is having enough readers and devoting enough time during the selection season to the search.

When should I apply?

Apply early in the fall before the year you want to begin, once you have assembled all the pieces of your application, including taking the LSAT and requesting your letters of recommendation and college certifications for those schools requiring them. Unless you are in a remote place, without access to a computer, you can begin the process of completing your application for submission and submit it electronically when you are ready. The admissions committee will not review your application until all required materials are received, so there is no advantage to rushing only to have the early components sit in the admissions office waiting for the additional pieces to arrive.

Will I have a better chance if I apply early?

Although most admissions officers will tell you that your chances are even at whatever time you submit your application, you will have your best chance if your application is in early. The vast majority of students apply electronically through Law Services, as is preferred by the vast majority of schools. When you file electronically, you select the schools to which you want your application sent and the questions you answer will cover everything each school has requested. Law Services then formats the answers and your essays and sends each school a paper copy which looks as if it were completed on the school's paper form. It is much easier for you and for the schools than if you fill out numerous forms and send them by mail to each school.

Your data will precede the application and other materials at the schools. The schools have access to your data as soon as you request that your application be sent there, and well before your actual application arrives. This gives them a head start on their work, as virtually all the data entry work is done. The school has data on all the applicants who have filed and have included them among the schools to which to send materials, and can compare the applicant pool to that of the previous year. The stronger applicants on average apply early in the year, taking the test in June, or no later than October. Therefore, although the data on later applications is unavailable for the early look at the pool, experience shows that the top of the pool takes shape early, enabling the start of admission and notification.

The elimination of huge amounts of paper work, and the ability to compare the early pool with the same point in previous years, facilitates making earlier decisions on some applications than might have been the case before electronic applications became the norm. If the shape of the pool should change later in the process, especially if it should become stronger than expected, your early application could yield an early offer of admission, whereas the same application sent later might have been wait-listed or even denied. If the later pool is weaker than anticipated, your early application might have been put aside early, and a later one admitted, but still your early application is likely to result in an offer of admission as soon as it is clear what the overall pool looks like.

If you apply early, you can save money because you will probably hear most of your decisions by early spring. If you hear from all your schools before tuition deposits are due, you can pay a tuition deposit only at your top choice among those admitting you, instead of forfeiting cascading deposits as later offers from your more preferred schools come in. If you are placed on hold, or wait-listed at your top choice, you may have to pay again, but most early applicants receive enough final decisions to lose no more than one tuition deposit.

How do early decision programs affect my chances?

If you are absolutely certain which school is your top choice, and it has an early decision program, apply for it (after evaluating the caveats below). Such programs usually guarantee you a yes or no decision by a certain date, or at that time will place you in a group of applicants continuing under consideration for available slots later.

If you are a typical applicant to early decision programs, you are aiming for a school that is a "reach" for you. The advantage to you is that the school may prefer you over comparable candidates applying in the normal pool because of your stated indication that they are your first choice. You could get in early at a school that would have wait-listed you had you applied in the ordinary sequence. Even if you are placed in the group for later consideration, you will ordinarily be preferred over other similarly accomplished candidates because of your expressed preference for the school. If you apply as—and are admitted as—an early decision candidate, you save yourself from applying to any other schools, and can begin making definite plans for the coming year.

The schools offering these programs get something out of this arrangement or they would not offer them. They like them because they know that they have 100 percent yield on all those whom they admit. They also get some of their work out of the way early in the year. Because of the advantages they gain, they are often willing to take a chance on people who might otherwise be at the low edge of their admit group.

Some caveats: As part of gaining this preferred status, you will be asked to sign an agreement that you will attend this school if admitted by the date promised, and will withdraw any applications made to any other schools. Because of the binding nature of the program, apply to an early decision program only if you are sure that the law school is your top choice. If you are admitted within the agreed window of time, there is no room for you to change your mind if you later find that you prefer another law school. Every year, numerous applicants rue their choice to apply for early decision.

Another reason to be careful about early decision programs is financial. Your chances for a merit scholarship diminish at the school admitting you under an early decision program, because the school has nothing to gain from offering it to you. Merit scholarships are usually offered as incentives to very strong but uncommitted applicants, while early decision candidates are already committed to attend. If you happen to be a strong, rather than borderline, candidate for the school of your choice, holding off on the early decision program preserves the possibility of a merit scholarship.

What is the difference between early decision and early action?

While early decision programs are binding, early action programs will give you early consideration resulting in a yes, no, or maybe decision. You can apply for early action at more than one school. The advantage to you is that you know early that you have one or more admissions offers, but are not committed to any one school. You can limit your other applications to those schools that you might prefer to those offering you admission under early action. Another advantage is your ability to plan ahead once you have been admitted, while maintaining your eligibility for any merit scholarship programs the school has to offer.

Schools like these programs because, even though you are not committed, experience shows that you will begin to bond with the school as soon as you are admitted, and they can start to recruit you early in the post admissions process. The applicant pools for such programs typically range toward the top of the school's overall pool and the yield, although not 100 percent, is typically higher than that of the pool as a whole. The school gets some of their selection work out of the way early. They increase their overall applicant pools, and they have an early shot at recruiting candidates away from competing schools.

When will I hear a decision?

How quickly you will learn the outcome of your application depends on:

- how long before the deadline you submitted your file,
- how strong your application is compared to others in the school's pool,
- whether your application raises questions,
- how many readers there are,
- how long each one takes to review the files submitted to him or her.

The closer to the deadline you submit your application, the longer it takes to become complete and ready for review, because there are more applications in the queue ahead of it, waiting to be processed by the staff and sent for decision by the committee. If it is missing materials, that is another cause for delay.

At HLS, nearly 20 percent of applicants submit their applications in the last two weeks before the deadline. Those applicants might wait several weeks to see their applications become complete simply because of heavy volume. Then the application will wait in another queue to be read by the committee. Only those with very strong numbers might be expedited, reaching the committee sooner than the others.

At any point, applications with stronger numbers don't have to pass through several screenings before reaching the voting members of the committee. They typically receive decisions more promptly even if, once all factors are taken into account, they are not stronger than others with lower numerical indicators.

Not always does a person with a strong file get a quick decision, because it may raise questions, or readers may disagree about what the decision should be, necessitating another reader. It may also happen that your file is kept by one reader or another for a relatively long time for no good reason. There is little that you can do about this, other than check in with the admissions office if you have heard no word for two months after your application was sent to the admissions committee.

Applications in the middle of the numbers pool take longer to receive a decision. There may be questions, disagreements, and slow readers that delay the decision, but the most likely reason is the need to compare the applicant with others in the pool before reaching a final decision. If you are in the middle of the pack, you may receive a letter saying that your application is on "hold" (see "What does being on hold mean?" below) or that a decision is deferred to a later time, or you may hear nothing for a long time. Some schools will notify you of "hold" status by letter or email, others will not contact you until they reach a final decision or make up a formal wait-list.

If questions are raised by your application, you should receive some notification and a chance to answer the question or resolve the issue. Prepare to do this promptly if this circumstance arises.

What is "rolling admissions"?

Rolling admissions describes an incremental process of building a class. Unlike most colleges, which have an early decision or early action date and a normal date on which all applicants are notified of their decisions, the law schools notify their applicants on a continuous or rolling basis. Colleges typically build their classes by assembling a group larger than wanted and then trimming it around the edges to make it the right size and shape just before all decisions become available. Law schools typically build their classes from the inside out, or the top down, making and sending decisions as the applications pass through the committee.

Some of my colleagues like to call it "rolling notification." Clearly admitted and denied applicants are notified promptly. Those applications that are held for comparison with later applications might have a tentative decision on them, and notification is delayed until the comparison is made. The admissions dean monitors the process and notifies more applicants as more applications are read and the outcome becomes clear.

What does being "on hold" mean? And what can I do if that happens to me?

Many schools find applicants they would like to admit but, when they have a still sizeable portion of their pool to read, decide to put those applications aside until they have a chance to complete, or nearly complete, the reading of files. Those applications are placed "on hold," and the decision on them is deferred to a later time. Because of the time that has passed since the application which is "on hold" was submitted to the committee for a decision, the admissions office sends an interim letter or email to the applicants. If you receive this notification, there is still hope for admission, depending on how your application stacks up against the remaining unread applications. The ultimate disposition of the applications on hold varies from year to year. In some years, most get in or are placed on the wait-list. In others, virtually none get in.

If you are notified that you are on hold and you still hope to attend the school, this is a good time to add to your application. Express your continued strong interest in attending if admitted. If you are still in school, get your first term grades sent. If you have an additional recommender, particularly one who might be familiar with something you are doing currently, ask that person to send a letter on your behalf. If you have been involved in a new activity or have a new accomplishment to report, send a letter outlining what you want the committee to consider. If you have already been admitted to a school that you prefer, withdraw your application in the interest of the other candidates who are waiting.

Can I do anything to help my application after I have filed it?

Once you have filed your application, there is little to do until you receive a preliminary response. If you are still in school, and new grades come in, be sure to submit them as soon as possible through Law Services. You should receive notice when your application has been submitted to the admissions committee. It is then inaccessible for added materials until it has been circulated and a tentative or final decision reached.

If you are placed on hold, submit whatever you can to enhance your chances. If something spectacular happens like winning a Pulitzer Prize for your writing, or being chosen for a prestigious scholarship like the Rhodes or Marshall, or receiving a Summa on your undergraduate thesis, don't wait.

Send whatever documentation or notification is appropriate, and then call or write the Dean of Admissions to say what it is and that it is on the way. If it is important enough, they will want to take it into account as they consider your application. Do not do this for relatively inconsequential accomplishments as it may diminish the overall impact of your application.

What are the decision makers thinking about when they read my file?

Your real question is "what do I need to do or have to get in?" or "what is your school looking for?" The frustrating short answer to this is "it depends," or "we'll know it when we see it."

A more expansive answer might be helpful here. They are looking at you both as a whole person and as the sum of your parts, evaluating what you will bring to the class. It does depend, both on what is in your file, and what you add to the mix of people who will make up the class. In law school, you are likely to learn as much from your fellow students as from your teachers and your books; schools consider it important for each class to include in the mix people with wide-ranging backgrounds, experience, and expertise, as well as varied perspectives on issues. What makes you different from most other applicants can give you an edge, assuming that you have at least moderately competitive "basics." I will discuss both the quantifiable and non-quantitative "basics" in more depth in the chapters on those subjects.

The admissions committee seeks to build a class of the most talented people in the pool, with varied backgrounds and a multitude of perspectives so as to enhance the learning experience of all. The class shape should have a mix of undergraduate schools and of majors, geographic distribution, range in age and the kinds of experience represented, and substantial representations of women and minority students, with a few foreign students mixed in. Building a class for law school does not mean trying to find a tuba player, or a strong hockey or football player, as it might in college, or even someone who will run or act in a law school show. But it does mean trying to find people with experiences and perspectives different from the norm, and people with skills, talents, and expertise that will contribute to a rich class discussion.

When college admissions committees considered your file, they evaluated your accomplishments in high school and before, and what promise you held for the future, found primarily in your SATs. When law school admissions committees look at your file, your accomplishments include everything you did in college and whatever you have done since you graduated. They evaluate those accomplishments in the context of your opportunities and of the obstacles that you have overcome to get where you are. They also look at where you are on the spectrum of your development and your life cycle.

The older you are and the more achievements you have, the less important are the numerical predictors. For a young person fresh out of college, whatever accomplishments you have to that point will be weighed along with your academic predictors. Sometimes the reader will project what you might do based on what you have done to date. For someone years out of college, accomplishment trumps potential, even the LSAT as a measure of potential. Whatever you have done to date will play a larger role than what you might do, given your background.

Don't underestimate the context of your opportunities. If you are the son of a congressman and think that serving as a congressional aide will give you a leg up, think again. If you come from an advantaged background, you should certainly take advantage of whatever opportunities present themselves, but you will be judged not on having experienced the opportunity, so much as what you did with it. Taking advantage of your opportunities and turning them into a contribution to your community might help your case.

If you have overcome obstacles to accomplish what you have done, be sure to make that known in your application. If you can have that corroborated by a recommender who has observed it personally, that is appropriate and helpful. Obstacles might include socioeconomic or educational disadvantage, including having to work full-time while you are in school. Or it might be a family tragedy or other personal hardship that took place while you were in high school or college. Don't consider a broken heart from an ended love affair as such an event—this is considered a normal part of growing up and claiming it or a broken leg as an obstacle will diminish more legitimate claims you might have.

Many decision makers evaluate your numerical credentials to see if they fit into the framework of the rest of the class. Will admitting you lower the average GPA or LSAT they report to the ABA and which are used by ranking groups to evaluate law schools? Although not a factor at every school, the pressure placed on the admissions officers and committee members by Deans ambitious to move up in the rankings, so as to attract more applications and better students, more alumni dollars, better jobs for future students, etc., is widespread and heavy. Only a few escape this reality. Unfortunately, those who judge and evaluate you may also be judged and evaluated by you after they admit you, for the same type of wrong reasons, which I discussed in more depth in the chapter on rankings.

Another facet that decision makers at some schools are considering as they read your file is the likelihood that you will attend if accepted. Incredibly, some schools are so worked up about the rankings that they try to minimize the number of offers they make that they are reasonably sure will not be accepted. You may find yourself targeted to show your interest by one or more of your back-up schools because the probability that someone with your credentials will accept an offer at the school is low. If you are asked to write an additional essay, or some other step is asked of you to demonstrate your sincere interest in the school, there is a chance that they don't believe you would accept an offer that is made. You can gauge the chance based on whether this school is one where you have a high probability of being admitted based on your numbers. If you really want to go there, do what they ask and the likelihood is that you will get in.

What does "holistic" mean?

When you ask how your application will be looked at it, most schools will tell you that they review applications in a holistic way. What does that really mean? When a school says that it takes a holistic view of each applicant, this means that rather than giving a certain number of points for LSAT, GPA, letters of recommendation, extracurricular and community activities, and personal statement, and adding them up to decide whom to admit, the reader looks at the application as a whole and votes to admit based on an overall impression of all factors taken together and in the context of one another. Some successful applicants will have outstanding academic records, some will have outstanding potential as measured by the LSAT, some will demonstrate outstanding leadership capabilities through their involvement in extracurricular and community activities, and some will demonstrate extraordinary promise for making a difference in the lives of others by their work in public service. A few applicants will have great strength in a variety of areas; some will have overwhelming strength in just one area, while presenting solid credentials in others. Some will have a history of poor testing, but exceptionally strong performance. Each applicant has his or her own distinctive qualities and the combination of these present a picture of what the person would bring to the table as a member of the class.

Taking a holistic view of applications also means that the committee is taking a holistic view of the class that comes from the applicant pool. You are not just a whole person made up of parts, you may also be part of a whole group that makes up a class. What you bring to the class may be something that is special about you, including an accomplishment of an academic or extracurricular nature, an area of expertise from your academic or work experience, or the way in which you handled adversity.

It takes experienced judgment by the decision makers to evaluate each set of credentials and place them in the context of the class under construction. Naturally, knowledge of previous classes at the school and of previous candidates, as well as of the other candidates in the particular pool, is essential to the process.

How do I make my application stand out?

A lot of candidates try different ways to stand out in the process. Don't do as these applicants did:

- Harry sent a racing shoe, with a note that with one foot in the door, he wanted to get the other in. The other had been sent to Yale, as we later found out. His shoe, or a picture of it, made it into our alumni magazine as an example of the strange things that applicants sent to the admissions office, but he did not make it into the class. I don't know how many shoes were received by admissions offices around the country and maybe his technique worked somewhere, but I don't recommend it.
- Robert sent us a sandal he had made, with the comment that he hoped we liked his "sole." The sandal was OK, but the committee didn't see it as a way to see through to his soul and there was no good result for him.
- Susie found out when and where our admissions committee met and had a singing telegram and balloons delivered. The telegram was about how much she wanted to attend the school. It went over as if the balloons were lead.

- Wendy did a body painting of herself and handwrote her personal statement in crayon around the edges. She did also submit the statement in the standard typewritten form. She actually got into a very good school, but not into others where a more conventional personal statement might have been enough. She got no points for her creativity, although she turned out to be a fine law student.

Also, don't send a videotape. For a while after the release of *Legally Blonde*, we received an increased number of videotapes, none of which we watched. Our committee bore no resemblance to the committee depicted in the movie. One year, as an experiment after the admissions season was over, our staff looked at a sampling of the videotapes and found that, almost universally, they would have harmed the application of the sender. Efforts to make yourself stand out often do not work, or can work to your disadvantage. Rest assured that you will stand out if, in presenting yourself in a simple, straightforward way, you demonstrate special accomplishments or attributes that are truly unusual or outstanding. Don't hesitate to highlight what is important, but don't let a gimmick get in the way of reality. Cleverness might have worked at the college level, but it won't fly at a law school.

Does the fact that my father, mother, or both parents went to the law school I am applying to help my case?

If one or both of your parents attended the law school in question, you may be considered a legacy applicant. If your parent or parents have been involved as alumni, there may be a bond that the school will take into account as they consider your application. If your application is strongly in the zone of serious consideration, you may get the nod. At the same time, if you are the first in your family to attend college, let alone law school, you may have an equal advantage as a bootstrapper, someone who has made it entirely on your own.

FINAL THOUGHTS

I hope this peek behind the scenes has lifted the curtain for you, or at least made it more transparent. Armed with the answers to basic questions and with some understanding of how admissions decisions are made, you should now be read to tackle the individual components of the application, beginning with the Law School Admissions Test. In the next few chapters, as we consider each component, we can address more complex questions and make each step a little less daunting.

CHAPTER NINE

The LSAT

THE LSAT IS TO law school what the SATs and ACTs are to college, a standardized test designed to measure the proficiency of applicants to law school in certain skills considered important to success in law school and lawyering. These skills are by no means the only important skills, but they are the most "testable." The LSAT is made up of five multiple choice sections, of which four are graded and the fifth is used to pretest questions and item types. At the end of these sections is a thirty-five minute writing sample, which is sent ungraded to each law school to which the applicant has applied. It is up to them to decide how to use it.

The LSAT was designed in the late 1940s to help top law schools to distinguish among otherwise similarly qualified applicants, and it has undergone numerous changes since that time. As the only standardized measurement in the admissions selection process for law schools, and the only factor required of virtually all applicants, the LSAT has assumed an importance in the admissions process far beyond what was intended by those who created it.

In the late 1960s, the LSAT increased in importance, when the volume of applicants began to mushroom and the admissions selection process became more rigorous. The demand for legal education has not abated. There may have been periodic fluctuations in the number of applicants to law school, but the demand has continued to exceed supply, even with the increase in the number of law schools.

As ranking systems like *U.S. News* have become prominent in evaluating law schools, the LSAT has become important to how schools are viewed and compared to one another.

Because of the demand for places in law school and because it is the only means of comparing you to all other applicants, your test score has become the most important factor in admissions, and subject to misuse in the selection process. Most applicants see it as the single most important obstacle to overcome in their quest for admission to a good, better, or "top" school. The combination of its importance and potential for misuse has rendered it a target for criticism.

HOW MUCH DOES YOUR SCORE COUNT?

It depends. There is no one answer to this question, nor is the answer quantifiable. For some applicants and for some schools, it matters a lot. For other applicants and other schools, the particular score may matter very little.

Although the LSAT is not used to the exclusion of other considerations, it is probably the most important factor at many schools. Yet, if you have a lot of other attributes going for you, particularly a very strong academic record, the LSAT diminishes in importance.

Having said that, the LSAT matters more than many schools will let on. Primarily because of pressure to respond to the challenge presented by ranking systems for law schools, admissions deans and committees have become more attentive to LSAT scores, and conscious of how admitting an applicant with a low score could affect their school's ranking. This is slightly less true at the top schools, but even at these pressures build as they compete with one another for top students.

Applicants tend to think the LSAT trumps all other factors, but it counts less than you think. It counts differently for different applicants, depending what else is in your file. Periodically, I reviewed the number of applicants with the top score on the LSAT to see what proportion was admitted. It turned out that less than 40 percent of applicants to HLS with the top score were actually admitted. For those denied, the other aspects of their files were not particularly strong, or the application raised questions for the committee. At the same time, there were substantial numbers of people with much lower scores admitted on the strength of other factors.

HOW DO SCHOOLS MISUSE THE LSAT?

The LSAC publishes Cautionary Policies for use of the LSAT that include warnings against using it as a sole criterion, placing excessive weight on score differences, and improper use of cut-off scores, below which the school will not consider an applicant for admission. They encourage schools to perform validity studies to evaluate the predictive ability of the test and to understand its limitations as a predictor. The LSAT is considered valid only for predicting performance in the first year in law school, and schools are urged not to share them with employers. Once first year grades are in, actual performance replaces predicted performance.

Schools are also advised to carefully evaluate scores that are earned under accommodated or nonstandard conditions. Tests are administered to persons with disabilities under these conditions and cannot be compared directly to those earned under standard conditions.

The Cautionary Policies were developed to respond to misuse of scores by schools. The main ways that schools misuse the LSAT are by putting too much emphasis on it to the exclusion of other factors and by paying too much attention to small differences in scores. LSAT scores are approximate rather than precise indicators of an applicant's potential for success in law school, and are reported to schools in "score bands" to remind the schools that the score could have been two or three points higher or lower, based on the standard error of measurement. But as schools work to achieve the highest possible 75th and 25th percentiles to report to the ABA and to ranking organizations, some admissions committees and deans will succumb to the temptation to admit an applicant with a score just one point higher than another, regardless of what other factors in the files would indicate about relative qualifications. Most state schools must answer to their legislatures about how the scarce resource of admission to law school has been allocated. It is a lot easier to point to a standardized number than to explain how the admissions committee made a complex judgment that favored one applicant over another.

HOW IS YOUR SCORE WEIGHED AGAINST OTHER FACTORS IN THE ADMISSIONS PROCESS?

If you took significant numbers of pass/fail courses in college, the LSAT will have a greater impact on your file than will your grades. If your academic record is weak or uneven or if you have been out of college for some time, your score will play a larger role in the admissions decision. If your academic record, extracurricular accomplishments, and work experience are very strong, a weaker LSAT will carry less weight, and a stronger one might just assure your admission.

If your college record has flaws beyond large numbers of pass/fail courses, a strong LSAT will probably help. This is particularly true if your overall record is not strong because of one bad semester or a handful of courses with which you had difficulty. It is also true if your grades rose dramatically from freshman year or after a sophomore slump. The overall record might look much weaker than that of the last two years.

If you are from a disadvantaged educational background, if English is your second language, or if you have a history of poor testing followed by a very strong performance in school, the admissions committee is more likely to discount a weak score. A strong score under these conditions carries much more weight in helping your application. If any conditions are true for you, inform the law schools to which you are applying, documenting what you can.

For example, if you have a history of poor testing, send a copy of your SAT or ACT scores along to document it. If you do not have that documentation in your own hands, your prelaw adviser or some other administrator at your college might have access to it and be willing to send it along for you. If you are an immigrant from a non-English-speaking country, send documentation of your arrival in the United States. In this circumstance, both the language barrier and the inexperience with U.S.–style standardized tests are mitigating factors for a mediocre score.

HOW DOES YOUR SCORE RELATE TO YOUR ACADEMIC RECORD?

Your LSAT is more predictive of performance when combined with or viewed in the context of your academic record. By itself, it may be a better predictor than any other factor, but that predictive ability typically rises dramatically when the score is combined with your academic record. Most schools use an index, combining grades and scores with a certain weight given to each, which is based on the results of a validity study. The validity study compares the prediction of performance arrived at by a combination of grades and scores with actual performance. The previous year's prediction was based on performance of the last group of students evaluated. The cycle continues from year to year with adjustments based largely on previous performance.

Some schools will make changes to their indices after each validity study. Others will make changes only if there is a dramatic shift in the contributions of grades or scores to prediction. The index is designed to provide some guidance to readers of the application not only in terms of overall prediction of performance between the two quantitative measures, but also with respect to how much relative weight should be attached to each of the quantitative predictors. (I will have more to say on this when I discuss the academic record.)

HOW TO PREPARE FOR THE LSAT

The first issue to address with respect to taking the LSAT is what you need to do before taking the test. To prepare or not to prepare? That is not really the question. The question of preparing for the LSAT should not be one of whether but how to do it. Do not take the LSAT on a whim, or without adequate preparation. Only a very rare bird stands to do well without preparation and that bird would probably do even better if it takes the time to prepare. You can prepare on your own, or you can sign up to take a prep course. There are a myriad of such courses, ranging from high-profile, expensive courses to low-profile free or low-cost courses guided by prelaw advisers.

Occasionally, I surveyed the entering class at HLS on a variety of subjects, including whether they had taken a prep course for the LSAT. Typically, the class split 50/50 on whether they prepared on their own or with a prep course. But the important point is that virtually all of them prepared!

If you need the discipline provided by a teacher going over the questions with you and administering the sample tests under testing conditions, and you are willing to pay well over $1000 to take the course, you may be a candidate for one of the high-profile prep courses. Simply paying the money can provide the incentive to make the most of your investment.

If your prelaw adviser offers a program, by all means take advantage of it. If you have a good study partner, or a friend or roommate who will beat you over the head to get you to sit down and take the sample tests under timed conditions, or you have the discipline to do it for yourself, you are a good candidate to prepare on your own. Keep a regular schedule of practice testing and work through tests until you feel very comfortable.

If you think paying for the course is the sole reason that you will practice, you could even pay your friend/roommate $50 or $100 to administer tests to you on a regular basis. It is worth giving it a try on your own, even if you do ultimately decide to take a prep course. You will get more out of the course if you have done some work on your own.

To help you prepare, LSAC has a test available online with explanations. It also offers copies of the most recent, disclosed tests for $8 each, batches of ten older tests for about $20, and a book called *The Official LSAT SuperPrep* with three disclosed tests and explanation of the answers to each question for $20. The high-priced prep courses buy these books in bulk and use them in their courses. Any books that have made up questions that purport to mimic the LSAT are probably not worth the money.

Different item types require different preparation. The test consists of one reading comprehension section, two sections of logical reasoning, and one section of analytical reasoning.

The *reading comprehension* section consists of three 450 word passages and one part with two shorter passages adding up to 450 words, used for comparative reading. Each passage has five to eight questions. Try various strategies to find your best and most efficient approach. Some people do better reading the questions first and then the passage while keeping the questions in mind, answering the questions after reading both. Others work through from the beginning, reading the passage carefully and then attacking the questions. Some fast readers will skim the whole thing before going back and reading closely while answering the questions.

Given that the test is speeded and you have limited time in the test, it makes sense to try different ways to see what works best for you. Once you are comfortable with your strategy, stick to it and practice, practice, practice.

The *analytical reasoning* section is nicknamed the logic "games" section. For many applicants, this is the most challenging section. A fortunate few find it easy and fun. It is designed to test your ability to understand the structure of complex relationships among people, places, things, amounts, etc., and to answer questions about them from a given set of rules, conditions, or statements. The relationships can be assigning, ordering, grouping, and arranging the subjects in time and space. They can be fixed or variable relationships. A simple example might be a family holiday gathering where some members should not be seated together, and others should be. Your analytical ability is tested by your answers to multiple choice questions about what is possible or impossible in the seating arrangements after taking into account a set of complicated criteria, including such things as who should sit to the left or right of someone in the group, and the like. Specific examples of this question type are given on the LSAC web site.

To practice this question type, you could try highlighting important words that describe or limit the relationship, and using diagrams to visualize the relationships. Here again, preparation involves developing your own system for responding to the questions.

There are two logical reasoning sections on the test, designed to test your ability to understand the point or issue described in a short passage, analyze and critique arguments, draw reasonable conclusions, and resolve conflicting arguments or facts. Each passage involves one or two questions. All the information needed to answer the questions is contained within the passages. To prepare, practice carefully reading short passages and, when answering the questions, focus only on the information contained in the passages. Don't bring to your answers any outside knowledge you possess.

At the end of the test is a thirty-five minute writing sample. You read a short passage and make a decision about some aspect of the topic and write an argument explaining your decision or point of view. There is no right answer, but your arguments should refer directly to the original passage.

Although some schools pay little or no attention to the writing sample, you don't want to take the chance that your top choice won't. Some schools who claim not to pay much attention to it will spot check, and others will use it as a diagnostic to determine which students will need help in developing their writing skills. Writing is valued in the legal profession and in law school. Even if you are hoping for extra help with your writing in law school, this is not the best way to get it.

Take the writing sample seriously. The writing sample shows what you can do under controlled conditions and provides a stylistic comparison to your personal statement. Trying to stand out or be cute could do you in. Don't use the writing sample to rail against the LSAT. Don't have a pre-prepared essay on some other topic just to fill the page. And don't just write one sentence or gibberish. Don't write about how much you love your teddy bear. All of these things have been done, and they showed enough poor judgment or attitude that more than one law school saw fit to deny admission on that basis.

To prepare, you should practice taking one position or another with sample passages as a way of practicing. Determine your own best strategy. Take up to half the time organizing your thoughts and outlining your answer. You will likely come up with arguments on both sides, and you can use the ideas on the side you do not choose as a foil for the arguments you make. The quality of what you write is more important than the quantity. It is better to write something incomplete well than to have a complete statement that is disorganized and sloppy.

Accommodations for applicants with disabilities

If you are an applicant with a documented disability, you may be eligible to take the test under nonstandard conditions. Those conditions include extra time on the test, rest periods between sections, and assistance from readers or writers. On the LSAC web site, click on "LSAT," then "accommodated tests" to see what you need to do. A diagnosis of a disability does not guarantee any particular accommodation, but once you have submitted the application for accommodations, the LSAC will review your request, make a decision about what they can do for you, and make the appropriate arrangements.

Strategies for taking the test

Eat right for at least a few days before the test, even if you don't typically watch how you eat. Get a good night's sleep the night before. Get up in time to have a good breakfast and leave plenty of time to get to the test site early. If you are not familiar with where the test will be administered or if there might be parking problems, leave even more time. If possible, go in the days before the test to scope out any potential issues.

When you get into the test, follow the strategies you have practiced. Answer every question, as there are no penalties for incorrect answers. There are no "trick" questions on the LSAT. All are designed to distinguish the most able from the less able students. If you find a difficult question, don't look up and be distracted by other test takers who are feverishly filling in all the boxes on the answer sheet. Don't let your life pass before you at that point, dwelling on what your life will be like if you don't do well on the test. There will be plenty of time for that after you leave the test site. Stay focused and skip over the difficult question. You can come back to it if you have time at the end of the section. It is far better to answer most of the questions without guessing than to be slowed by one question so that you are guessing on the easier ones. When you skip over a question, be sure to leave the space for its answer vacant on your answer sheet to avoid the problem of misgridding, or putting the right answers in the wrong boxes. Give yourself at least thirty seconds at the end of the test to go back and guess on any unanswered questions.

If you have a "bad feeling" after you take the test

It is possible that you will come out of the test totally wiped out. You may feel that the test was much more difficult than you had anticipated, and that you did not do well, or at least not as well as you had hoped. You may hear others talking about the test as if they found it much easier than you did, or they may mention a question with which you had difficulty and chosen a different answer. You have one week after the test to decide if you want to cancel your score. If you cancel your score, two things will happen.

First, you will never know what your score was on the test and second, you will have to take the test again. Think carefully about the factors going into the decision to cancel your score. If you had great difficulty focusing because of an internal or external distraction that is unlikely to be repeated, like the school band playing outside or the person next to you becoming ill, or you have experienced a personal trauma like a serious illness or a death in the family in the few days before the test, the test conditions might be your own personal issue, and there might be good reason to consider canceling your score.

If you simply found the test more difficult than you thought, it may be that there were more difficult questions on the particular test you took. Less able students than you might not have recognized they were difficult questions. Because questions are equated across tests, the presence of a higher percentage of more difficult questions might mean that the scores will run higher on that test than on others where the questions are easier. I vividly recall one year when a relatively large number of very able applicants cancelled their scores on a particular test. It turned out that it was a test with many difficult questions; and those able students who cancelled their scores would actually have scored very high.

WHAT TO DO AFTER THE TEST RESULTS COME OUT

What if you didn't cancel your score and when you get your test results, you are very disappointed? Unless you took a version of the test that is not disclosed, which is true of only one administration each year, you will get a copy of the answer sheet with your own answers charted against the correct ones The first thing that you should do is to look carefully at the correct answer sheet against your own answers. See what you did wrong.

Did you misgrid? You can tell if you did by seeing if there is a pattern of incorrect answers where your answers are just one question away from the correct answers for a stretch. If that is the case, you may want to contact Law Services to request a hand scoring of a section or the whole test.

Should you take the test a second time? A third time?

After you have completed the review of your test results, you may wonder whether taking the test again will significantly improve your chances of admission to the school you most want to attend. As my colleague Dick Badger of University of Chicago law school likes to say, paraphrasing Dr. Samuel Johnson, taking the test a second time is like "a second marriage, a victory of hope over experience." You may have hope that your second test will come out better than your first, but the experience of most applicants is that it does not, or at least the results are so little different that it does not make a difference in admissions probabilities. Studies based on applicants who have taken the test multiple times show that the true score lies slightly above the average of tests taken. Should your score go down, your average will fall below your first test score.

If you are seriously considering taking the test a second time, consider what you concluded from your review of your experience in the first test, and from the results. If the conditions were bad, or your mind was distracted, consider whether these circumstances are likely to repeat themselves. Did you fail to finish? Were you distracted by a difficult question? Can you find something that is unique to this testing? If there was a unique distraction, you may want to consider taking the test again.

Consider whether you were adequately prepared and then whether further preparation might make a difference. Check whether your scores are substantially different from how you scored on the SAT, particularly the math portion. If they are very different, that is an argument for repeating the test. If none of these conditions are met, you are probably better off with your first score.

FINAL THOUGHTS

Remember that your LSAT score is important, but not by itself determinative, with respect to the decision on your application. If you have prepared to the best of your ability and given careful consideration to the question of retaking the test before deciding whether to do so, you have given it your best shot, and it is time to move on to the other pieces of your application.

CHAPTER TEN

GPA and Academic Record

THE OTHER QUANTIFIABLE FACTOR in your application is your GPA. This factor represents your academic record and it is only approximately quantifiable. As Rick Geiger, my colleague from Cornell, likes to say, "Not all 3.5 GPAs are equal." There are three factors which make the same GPA different. The first is the quality of the undergraduate school at which the GPA was achieved. The second is the grading practices at different undergraduate schools or in different departments at the same school—at some schools, grades are inflated more than at others, and even within schools, some departments grade more rigorously than do others. The third is the rigor of—and skills developed in—the individual courses on the transcript of grades. Other considerations are the trend in grades and the distribution of courses, the evidence of skills developed, and the nature and substance of the courses taken. I will discuss these in more depth in the sections that follow.

QUALITY OF UNDERGRADUATE SCHOOL

Where you earned your undergraduate degree can influence the evaluation of your GPA. If you went to one of the most prestigious undergraduate schools, your grades were earned in competition with other very talented individuals. You and your fellow students won the national competition for admission at the college level and during college you competed with one another. The law schools will reach more deeply into your class to take students, and students from your school with lower GPAs than those of students from lower-ranked schools will have a higher probability of admission.

An indicator that admissions deans and committees use to evaluate the quality of undergraduate schools is calculated for them by LSAC. It is called the LSAT College Mean (LCM), and is the average LSAT score for all students from that undergraduate school who took the LSAT and applied to law school over the past three years. Calculated for any college with enough applicants to law school for the mean LSAT to provide helpful information, it will appear on your LSDAS report, which will be sent to you and to the law schools to which you apply. The LCM tracks well with the various rankings of undergraduate schools.

GRADING PRACTICES

Grading practices at undergraduate schools are also tracked by LSAC for applicants to law schools, and another number is generated. This is the GPA College Mean (GCM) which represents the average grade point average for students from that undergraduate school who have applied to law school over the past three years. The GCM appears on the LSDAS report, along with another related number. This is the GPA percentile rank, which tells the admissions reader the applicant's percentile rank compared with the other applicants from that school who have applied to law school over the past three years. Note that this is not your actual rank in class, just your relative position vis a vis the three year grouping of applicants to law school from your undergraduate school.

What the two pieces of data tell the admissions reader is the extent to which grades are inflated at the school and where the applicant stands in comparison with others from that school.

To give you an idea of how the LCM, the GCM, and the GPA percentile rank work together to help compare applicants, let's look at the example of Bob and Dick, twin brothers who were both admitted to top undergraduate schools, but decided to go to different ones.

Bob decided to go to California to attend Stanford, while Dick wanted to stay closer to home on the East Coast, and decided to attend Swarthmore. Both schools are outstanding, and it happens that they both have about the same LCM. Both young men decided to go to law school after graduating, and both did pretty well on standardized tests. They got the same score when they took the LSAT. Both had excellent extracurricular activities and similar jobs during the summer, with very good recommendations from their teachers and their employers.

The main difference in their candidacy was that Bob had a 3.55 average at Stanford, whereas Dick had only a 3.33 average at Swarthmore. So it would seem that Bob would be the stronger applicant, and would be admitted more readily to more law schools.

But it turns out that grades have not inflated at Swarthmore very much, whereas the grades at Stanford run very high. At Swarthmore the average applicant has below a 3.2 average, while at Stanford, the average applicant has better than a 3.5 average. So actually Dick's academic record is stronger, and he has a better shot at admission than does his brother, because all the admissions readers have access to information about the relative strengths in schools and the relative performance of students at the different schools.

TRANSCRIPT OF GRADES

Beyond the quantitative adjustments to grades calculated in the mind of the reader who is considering your application for admission to law school are some non-quantifiable factors that modify their thinking about your academic record.

After you apply, you will receive a copy of your LSDAS report, showing how your grades have been summarized and presented in a 4.0 system, giving you the LCM, the GCM, and your percentile rank at your school You won't receive a copy of your actual transcript, but the law school admissions offices will, and it will become the primary focus of their attention as they consider your academic record. They will examine the transcript for a variety of attributes, the first of which is the rigor of the courses taken. Beyond the obvious rigorous course types like hard sciences, engineering, computer science, and math, there may be other courses that you want to highlight as especially rigorous at your school. If you attended one of the major feeder schools for the law school that is looking at your file, the reader will have substantial experience with applicants from your college and will be well versed in most or all of the courses that appear on your transcript.

Knowledge of major feeder schools and their curricula is one of the skills that professional admissions officers develop. If your school is not well known to most law schools, you may want to ask one of your faculty recommenders to call attention to courses that are more rigorous than they might appear to someone unfamiliar with your school.

The reader will also be looking at the content of your courses. Beyond degree of difficulty, some courses have content that is particularly useful for some fields of the law, even though most top law schools will consider the development of skills more important. They will look for evidence that you have developed the reading, writing, and analytical reasoning skills that will help you with the study of law.

In the quest for relevant course content, don't get sucked into the idea of a major in criminal justice or "prelaw." They are majors that make admissions deans, at least from the top schools, cringe. They are in the league with elementary education, performing arts, musical performance, studio arts, hotel management, and physical education: worthy for their own purposes, but not good indicators of potential success in law school.

BREADTH AND DEPTH OF COURSEWORK

Breadth and depth of coursework is both a demonstration of skills development and evidence of intellectual curiosity and willingness to venture outside your comfort zone. Your transcript should show depth in at least one area of study to a high level, possibly including independent work.

Writing a senior thesis can be a good demonstration of depth of coursework. The decision to write one should be made only because of genuine interest in the subject, because it may come at the expense of exploring completely new fields. Working outside your area of expertise and finding ways to synthesize it with work in your field can demonstrate potential for applying your legal studies. Writing a thesis can also help distinguish an otherwise undistinguished transcript, but showing that you can do good work outside your comfort zone can do the same. Both have value, and you should choose whichever works best for you. If you can do both, all the better. Students who are ready, willing, and able to take on intellectual challenges tend to be more appealing than those who have better grades, but did not venture very far beyond their majors.

Does a double major show both breadth and depth of coursework? It depends. Double majors and interdisciplinary majors are two ways to demonstrate expertise in more than one area. If that is what you have chosen to do, make the most of the multiple areas of expertise that you have. The problem with double majors is that they leave less room to take courses outside the chosen subjects. The interdisciplinary major builds in a certain amount of breadth, but it too can leave you with less flexibility to balance your academic experience.

TRENDS IN GRADES

The admissions reader will also be interested in your trend in grades. An upward trend in grades is always better, although a strong start even without an upward trend bears a strong relationship to how you might fare during your first year in law school.

A weak overall record with a very strong last two years will in most cases be favored over a slightly stronger record that is flat throughout because of the attraction to late bloomers. Other patterns worthy of mention are the sophomore slump, interrupted schooling, change of major—especially the "premed exit"—and transfer between four year colleges or from a community college.

The typical sophomore slump occurs after a strong freshman year and precedes a strong junior and senior year. Sophomore year is the most common time for an otherwise strong college student to lose motivation or direction, with a resulting drop in grades. It is almost always a temporary situation. It can happen to you as late as second semester sophomore year or even during junior year, when you realize that graduation is just around the corner, and you have not yet found your passion or even excitement in academic work. Not unlike an anomalous grade or two in an otherwise strong transcript, the sophomore slump is one of the factors that admissions readers consider normal when evaluating the overall record. The overall GPA might be affected but, like an upward trend in grades, the overall is considered better than one with the same GPA that is flat throughout.

A severe sophomore slump or some other upset to your educational momentum can result in an interruption of your schooling, sometimes for several years. Usually this produces a bifurcated record, or the equivalent of two different records making up the whole.

Betty started out in college too young, and when her mother became ill during her freshman year, she was distracted and did not do as well as she was able. Her mother was adamant that she stay in school, so she did, but she traveled home every weekend to see her mom. When her mother died during her sophomore year, Betty went into a tailspin and stopped doing the work in her courses. She tried to recover and take her exams, but did very poorly. She dropped out at the end of spring semester and stayed at home adjusting and helping her dad with her younger brother and sister, until they were ready to go to college.

Working as a salesperson in a local clothing store allowed her to have flexible hours, and she did well. She was promoted to department manager and considered a career in retail sales management. But gradually she became motivated to return to college. As a young woman in her late twenties she achieved a 4.0 average, and developed an interest in public interest law through volunteer work she did with at-risk teenagers. Her overall record, thanks to the false start, is about 2.66.

With the personal hardships that Betty has overcome, and with a recent record that is outstanding, it is likely that most law schools will ignore her earlier record, even though her overall GPA, if earned at one time under normal conditions would put her out of the running at the same schools.

Another type of two part record is nicknamed the "premed exit," to describe the premed students who discover that they do not like the sight of blood and they do not do very well in college level science courses. Biochemistry seems to be a major stumbling block for a lot of students who make premed exits. A major feature of the premed exit is a great improvement when the sciences are left behind for the social sciences or the humanities. It can signal the development of a real passion for the new subject, where the old one was undertaken out of a sense of obligation, study to be endured for the reward of becoming a physician.

David had expected to be a doctor ever since he was a young boy. His dad was a doctor as were his uncle and his cousin. Medicine was the family profession. David did well in science in high school, but when he got to college, he began to be interested more in medical care policy than in actually caring for patients. He had an internship in a hospital, and saw the frustrations the medical personnel faced. When he returned to college, his heart was not in his science courses and he did not do well in his organic chemistry class. The next summer he served an internship at the Department of Health and Human Services. With a newfound interest in health care policy, he took a couple of courses in political science and began to think that he could do more for the medical profession by working on the policy issues than by continuing coursework that did not interest him as much. His college work up to that point had been adequate, but not outstanding. After changing his major to political science, he started getting As where he had gotten Bs in his science courses, and the C in Organic Chemistry. When applying to law school, he realized that his GPA overall was a 3.33, although his work in political science was closer to a 3.8.

David is the classic example of the premed student who realizes that he does not really want to practice medicine sometime

in the middle of his college career. Most admissions readers will give him the benefit of the doubt with respect to his work in the sciences, and will treat his record as if it were closer to the 3.8 work that he was doing after changing his major.

Other changes of major may be less dramatic, but sometimes other changes in major will have a positive impact, and sometimes students are just late bloomers in college. They do lackluster work as first, but once they find their passion, they take off!

Another way applicants show two separate records is to transfer from one college to another after one or two years at the first, or move from a community college to a four year college for the last two years. If you were unhappy at your first college, and you show dramatic improvement at your new school, the trend in your grades will be sharply higher at the new school. If, on the other hand, you have problems adjusting to the new school, your grades might take a hit your first semester or first year at the new school.

The same can occur in the transition from a two year to a four year college. Some students will rise to the top of the class with the extra stimulation provided at the four year school, and others will have difficulty getting acclimated to the new demands, the new surroundings, and the new set of classmates. The latter will take more time to do their best work.

In these cases the LSDAS report will show the summary GPA, which includes transcripts from all schools attended, as different from the GPA at the degree-granting institution, and the admissions reader will need to evaluate each situation individually. In most cases, the student will be given the benefit of the doubt, but generally the work at the second school carries more weight than that at the first. Ideal for those who flourish right away in the new environment, it is problematic for those who have difficulty making the transition.

One group of people who may not benefit in their applications from a rising trend in grades are the "intro specialists."

These students continue to take introductory courses into their junior and senior years. They may be getting plenty of breadth in their coursework, but they are certainly sacrificing depth. Competing with freshmen and sophomores in these courses, they may get the top grades, but they do not receive the full benefit of them in the law school admissions review because of the context in which they earned them. Further, the admissions reader is likely to be less impressed with the rigor of the coursework overall, and will at least slightly discount the GPA. If you must take an introductory course during your junior or senior year, balance it with a number of more advanced courses.

REDEMPTION OR REHABILITATION

What can you do if your record does not demonstrate your academic capability and you want to redeem yourself in the eyes of the admissions committee? Suppose your academic record is uneven and your GPA is below what most people admitted to the law schools you are interested in have achieved. At best, your record would be described as lackluster, and it is clearly the weak spot in your file. You've finished college and have decided you want to apply to law school. Is it too late to do anything to demonstrate that you will be an excellent student in law school? The answer here is that it depends.

The longer your record recedes into your past, the better your chances are that it will be less important to your probability of admission. The more significant and sustained work experience you can put between yourself and a mediocre academic record, the better. Many of my colleagues and I share the view that each applicant applies at a given stage of his or her development, a snapshot in time. If you can demonstrate that you are a more serious and accomplished person than you were as an undergraduate, you will do better than if you have moved from job to job with no real progress. If you have a significant work experience, you might have an opportunity to write reports or other works that have potential for publication. That might help with any questions about your writing ability. A very strong LSAT score will help a mediocre record by itself, but it too will be more effective as time passes since your graduation. A strong LSAT combined with a strong work record will help even more. As suggested in the section on Preparing Your Case, you may consider doing some graduate work to show that you are capable of strong academic work, but since grades are inflated in most graduate programs, you are unlikely to make much of a dent, unless your program is known for its rigor or for tough grading. It can make a little dent, however, and a detailed letter of recommendation from a teacher who can compare your work to that of others in a favorable light will help. The stronger the program, the more information about it, the bigger the dent it will make.

ANOTHER LOOK AT BUILDING YOUR ACADEMIC RECORD

If you still have time before your academic record is complete, take another look at the chapter on preparing your case. Take courses that will help you develop skills and to demonstrate your strength as a student. Eliminate those introductory or survey courses that you were saving for senior year and take something that will add dimension to the record you already have. If you are still in the early phase of your college education, follow the advice in the chapter on preparing your case while in college, and bear in mind the way your transcript is likely to be viewed as presented earlier in this chapter.

HOW TO ANALYZE YOUR OWN TRANSCRIPT

Looking at your own transcript with the admissions committee in mind can be a daunting task, but if you take each element described above separately and consider how it might be perceived individually before putting all the elements together, that can make your analysis more manageable. Once you receive your copy of the LSDAS report, you can see roughly how your school is perceived by looking at the LCM and the GCM, and you can see how you rank against your fellow alumni who were among applicants to law school during the last three years. You can then examine the coursework to see it as others might, and to determine whether any courses need explanation or elaboration. Look for grade anomalies, and for courses you have taken pass/fail. Did you start out as premed or in the sciences? Did you change majors? Did you transfer schools, and how did the transition go? What is your trend in grades and how steep is the incline or decline? If the trend is in the wrong direction, what made that happen?

Putting the best spin on your academic accomplishments

Once you understand your transcript from the perspective of the admissions committee, the next step is to decide what needs explanation and how to present it. Do not try to explain every little glitch or aberration. Choose those which are most important or most easily explained.

Don't whine! Always remember that admissions committees like a positive attitude and potential students who show that they can take charge of and responsibility for their education.

Some aspects of your transcript will be self-evident and if you made a simple premed exit or change of major, you can rely on the fact that the admissions reader will recognize the phenomenon without your calling attention to it. However, if there is a way to put a positive spin on your change, a simple description of your evolving interests is an effective way to note the change and turn the transition into a plus for your application.

If your school is not well known, and there are some courses that sound like fluff but are really tough, you might want to be sure that one of your recommenders talks about your school and your transcript in detail.

If you took many courses pass/fail, make sure you get a letter of recommendation from at least one of the professors, especially if there is one who can speak to the fact that you produced outstanding work in the course. If the trend in grades is in the wrong direction, you may explain, but never argue for an excuse.

FINAL THOUGHTS

The overall picture of your academic record is much more complex than any one of its parts or than the GPA that purportedly sums it up. It is in the law school's best interest to examine the record in all its complexity to determine the quality of your academic performance and assess your preparedness to flourish in its program. Understanding that complexity through careful consideration of the issues discussed in this chapter should help you to identify those issues, if any, to which you want to call the admissions committee's attention.

CHAPTER ELEVEN

Letters of Recommendation

LETTERS OF RECOMMENDATION CAN be key qualitative documents in your admissions file. Close to 99 percent of letters of recommendation for law school are positive, but the vast majority are not as effective as they should be. How do you make your letters of recommendation work for you, and make a difference in your probability of admission?

The best letters will be substantive and detailed about your academic ability and personal qualities, helping the admissions committee understand your academic accomplishments in context and appreciate you as a person and future member of their community. They clarify your academic record and explain anything that is significant in your record, filling any gaps in the picture the rest of your file paints of you. They provide a faculty member's perspective on your accomplishments highlighting particularly difficult courses, explaining a rigorous course selection if applicable, and clarifying any problem areas and any mitigating circumstances.

As you consider how to achieve the most advantage from your letters of recommendation, you should consider who is best equipped to write about you and how to help those persons present your case most effectively.

WHO SHOULD WRITE YOUR LETTERS?

Most schools prefer academic letters of recommendation, but which teacher is best suited to write one for you? Pick someone who knows you well. If you are still in the middle of your college education when you read this, choose a faculty member or two to get to know as preparation for asking for a letter of recommendation, teachers you really admire, and whose courses you genuinely enjoy. Take courses known to be rigorous and the professor demanding if possible.

It will be even better if the professor genuinely likes you. You can gauge this by working to get to know them, over lunch or at any event where you can talk to them informally. At the very least, go to his or her office hours armed with ideas or with good questions you developed by paying close attention in class. In making your choice, think about whether your potential recommenders are likely to write persuasively. You can judge this by reading their books or their comments on papers that you have written.

If the faculty members you choose are the type to write useful comments on your papers and exams, they are also likely to write detailed and substantive letters of recommendation. Ask for advice from upperclassmen or from previous successful applicants to law school from your college about who might write a good letter. By a good letter, I don't mean one that praises you. A good letter can actually be critical of you if they point out weaknesses overcome or perseverance in the face of difficulties encountered in the class, or from external events while taking the course. Someone known to be tough on students is usually a better choice than someone who is overly kind. Consider this tale of two teachers:

_____

Two professors from a top Ivy League college wrote many letters of recommendation for law school applicants. Both cared a lot about their students. One taught one of the most popular courses in the college, which sounded rigorous and broadening for the typical prelaw candidate. Almost everyone who took the course got an A, and everyone loved the professor, who was a wonderful person, totally dedicated to his students. Everyone who asked him for a letter of recommendation got a glowing, lengthy letter, offering the highest of recommendations. Everyone!

The other professor taught a rigorous set of courses in a common subject for future law students. Some students avoided his courses because he was a hard grader. Letters that he wrote for law school applicants critiqued the applicant, noting areas of weakness along with positive qualities and achievements; some students fared better than others under his scrutiny.

I saw many applicants from this school. Many more recommendations came from the first professor, but the second professor carried much more weight with my admissions committees. The high praise heaped on all his students by Professor One made it impossible to distinguish the really strong student from the average. The letters from this caring professor became virtually useless. The result was unfortunate because he put his best effort into finding the best things to say about each person.

From Professor Two, the relative strengths and weaknesses of the applicants for whom he wrote letters were clear, and we could pull the stars out of the pack. In some cases his letters completely reversed what the transcripts told us about comparable students and gave the truly gifted student an edge even where grades did not dictate such distinctions.

I was not alone in my reaction to the two recommenders, nor was this situation unique. For many years the recommendations from the Houses at Harvard College were notorious for heaping high praise on all candidates and making no distinctions among them. Some Houses now make those distinctions, but others cling to the idea that the letter is an important marketing tool for the students, and that every student deserves the strongest possible recommendation. My fellow admissions officers and I know which faculty members at the larger "feeder" schools write really useful letters, and which write letters that are not particularly helpful. We can read between the lines of many letters written by frequent writers.

A few give us guidance about how to read between those lines. In the search for the best academic letter be wary of the "famous professor syndrome." If you have done very well in the course of a very well-known and highly regarded professor, you may be tempted to seek a letter of recommendation from him or her. The mere fact that said professor was willing to write for you should speak for itself, but it does not. Unless the professor knows you well, and has indicated a special interest in you as a student, use caution in relying on him or her to write a really useful recommendation. The admissions deans will be able to see that you have done well in his or her class, but the very brief and bland letters that frequently emanate from such professors would add no luster to your application. There should be more to your relationship than that you did well in the course.

As a group your recommenders should span the areas that you most want to highlight, for example, one faculty recommendation from your major field and another outside. Once these bases are covered, choose someone who knows something about your activities or work experience, like the faculty sponsor of the organization if it is curriculum related, or the coach if you have made a major commitment to a sports team. Faculty members like these can talk about your character and the nature and importance of the activity through which you know them. They might cover such qualities as leadership, teamwork, integrity, judgment, concern for others, energy, sense of humor, and the like. All the better if you also took a course from them.

What about the utility of a letter of recommendation from an employer? Some of my colleagues welcome such letters for the additional dimension they add to what else they know about you. The more experience you have, the more relevant and appropriate a letter is likely to be. If your experience amounts to summer jobs, an internship here and there, and just having started work in a full-time job as you begin your applications to law school, hold off seeking a letter from an employer. If you had close contact in one of your summer jobs or internships with a highly regarded person who has credibility in the academic world, ask for an additional letter from this person, subject to the same conditions and preparation that you did with your academic recommenders. The more relevant to law are your work and the person who is writing the recommendation, the more useful the letter. The longer you have worked for the person, the better. If you spent all three college summers in the same organization working for the same person, and you advanced in your work each year, a letter is warranted. Otherwise, a full year of full-time work is appropriate before you request a recommendation from your supervisor.

Another important thing to note is that if you have worked for the same organization and the same person for several years, it will seem odd to the admissions committee if you do not include a letter from your employer. If you have not yet notified your employer of your application to law school, let the committee know why you have not requested a letter. If you have changed bosses, even if you are in the same job, get a letter from your previous supervisor. If you have changed jobs, a letter from a previous employer is good.

Another high-profile person from whom to resist requesting a recommendation is your congressman, senator, mayor, or any other elected official. Many law school applicants have served an internship with a congressman, senator, or some other elected official. It is rare for them to know your work well. Often letters signed by them are written by your immediate supervisor for the signature of the congressman or other official. Frankly, it shows that they have not written the letter themselves, and it doesn't reflect well on you. It would be better to have a letter signed by your immediate supervisor, who can speak to your contribution and to your abilities. There are exceptions to this: if you have worked closely with the elected official and you are sure they know you well enough to write a good letter, then you should get the letter. But even that may be subject to some skepticism because of the ubiquitous glowing, but vapid letters coming from such officials.

This brings me to one of the more delicate problems you may face in choosing a recommender. Some recommenders may offer to sign a letter of recommendation that you write for them. This may seem like a tempting opportunity to toot your own horn and have someone else take responsibility, but it can be extremely difficult to find the right words and tone to put in someone else's mouth. Chances are that you will overstate or, more likely, understate your own accomplishments, and that the letter will lack the feel of authenticity. Your own writing style might well show through. In short, you can shoot yourself in the foot with pretty serious consequences. Although the recommender, having invited you to do this, is unlikely to turn you in, he might receive a call from an admissions office, asking him questions about what he wrote, to his own—and your—embarrassment. Better to look for another recommender.

HOW TO GET THE MOST EFFECTIVE LETTER

The best and most effective letters of recommendation will describe you in such detail and such terms as to bring you to life for the committee. Very few letters achieve this. Still, a good letter will tell things about you that might not be evident elsewhere in your file, or will fill in gaps that it would be awkward for you to fill. To get the most effective letter from your chosen recommenders, you can help them.

The first thing to give them is time. Do not expect that they will be able to turn around a letter of recommendation in a week, let alone a day or two. Ask for your letters early in the term in the year in which you are applying, if you have not already requested the letter directly after the term in which you took their course. Since some schools will hold letters of recommendation in their files throughout your college career and well into your professional career, you may want to collect letters as you go along.

To get a specific and detailed letter for law school, schedule meetings with your recommenders, in which you provide them with as much information as you can impart in the time you have together. Even if you have a general letter on file from the same person, it is worth trying to get an updated one targeted at law school.

Before your meeting, size yourself up. What do you hope to highlight for the admissions committee? What can be best conveyed by someone other than you? Help organize their thinking by giving them copies of your transcript, your resume, and any paper you wrote for them, with their comments included if possible. To this add a statement describing what you hope to accomplish in your legal education and what you bring to the table to accomplish it, noting specifically those aspects that you hope will be highlighted in their letters.

Resist the temptation to give them a copy of your personal statement. I have read many recommendations that seem to paraphrase the personal statement, making it seem that either you wrote the letter for their signature or that they changed a few words here and there to write a more detailed letter than they might otherwise have done. If they ask you for your statement, prepare one that is different from the one you are submitting. Use the opportunity to highlight some aspect of your background or achievements that it is awkward for you to express directly in your application.

Alternatively, you might address some aspect of your application that you have not highlighted but which you want the committee to know about. Whatever these matters are should at least be mentioned in your file, although you may leave it to the recommender to expand upon them.

After your meeting, send a thank-you note, in which you summarize the major points of discussion, which you hope will find their way into the recommendation, and remind them of when you hope to have the letter of recommendation sent.

If you cannot arrange a meeting with any one of your recommenders, try to approximate the conditions of the meeting in an email or a letter. Be sure to give them the date by which you need the recommendation. Include all of the helpful documents and send a follow-up thank-you after a short time, asking if any further information would be helpful, and reminding them gently about the deadline.

Equipping your recommenders with your resume, your transcript, and your statement of aspirations, should put them in a good position to write a good letter, tying in what they know about you directly from your work with them with what they know about the campus. They can comment on your other courses, the rigor of your overall transcript, and the dimensions of your extracurricular involvements.

Your letters of recommendation are critical partners to your transcript in providing a full picture of your academic record. They can add clarity and dimension to the information on your transcript. They can explain with authority those aspects which you might have difficulty documenting, or add verification of what you say about it yourself.

LETTER OF RECOMMENDATION SERVICE (LORS) FROM LSAC

Yet another service offered by LSAC to streamline your multiple applications, and to assist the schools in their paperwork, is the Letter of Recommendation Service (LORS). Some schools require that you use this service and others recommend it. Only a small number will not accept letters by this route. It is your choice whether to use it unless you apply to schools which require it, and then you might as well add all other schools that recommend it.

You print out forms for your recommenders to use to attach to their letters, which they send by mail to LSAC. They need send only one letter for all your applications unless you request that they target letters to some schools. Give each recommender a pre-addressed stamped envelope to send the letter(s) to Law Services, demonstrating your organization and respect for their time. The form will have all your demographic information and a bar code to match with your other data and materials when it is received by LSAC.

You can have up to four general letters sent to all the schools to which you apply, and any number of targeted letters, to be sent to those schools your recommender indicates. You make the choice about targeted letters. A good example is a targeted letter from a professor who is an alumnus of one of the schools to which you are applying. Another is a recommender who has a specific relationship with a particular law school faculty member.

HOW MANY LETTERS OF RECOMMENDATION ARE TOO MANY?

The LSAC publishes a listing of all schools using their letter of recommendation service with the number of letters required and the number accepted by each school. As you request recommendations, remember that the schools will consider your application complete as soon as they have received the number they require. Beyond that number, ask them to wait for however many more you want them to consider. The more you ask them to wait for, the higher the probability that your application will be delayed by one laggard letter writer. Stay within the number accepted by each school. Going well beyond that number will be overkill, a distraction, and could lead to them questioning your judgment. Consider carefully the incremental value of each letter you request. A small number of well chosen letters is a sign of good judgment.

TO WAIVE OR NOT TO WAIVE YOUR RIGHT TO SEE THE LETTER?

In 1974, Congress enacted what is popularly known as the Buckley Amendment. Its formal name is the Family Educational Rights and Privacy Act (FERPA). Among its provisions is the right of any student to see copies of letters sent for admissions purposes to the school at which he or she is registered. This right is guaranteed unless you specifically waive it when you request that a letter be sent on your behalf to a school to which you are applying. You may be in a quandary as to whether to waive your right to see your letters. You may have had to make the same decision when you applied to college.

Law schools generally do not care whether you waive your right. The only issue for them is whether you will get a brief, bland letter with plenty of adjectives but no substance from recommenders who would write a more detailed letter if you have waived your right to see it. Make your own decision, bearing in mind that you can only see the letters at the school where you matriculate, and that there is a risk, albeit small, that your letter will be less substantive and therefore less effective if you do not waive your right to see them. Waiving your right shows you have confidence in your recommenders and what they will say about you.

FINAL THOUGHTS

How well your letters work for you depends on how well they support other aspects of your application, including your academic record and your experience. The thought and preparation you put into choosing your recommenders and then equipping them to talk about aspects of your academic and other experience both within and beyond what they know directly can greatly increase the value of those letters.

CHAPTER TWELVE

Extracurricular and Community Activities

B EYOND ENHANCING YOUR ACADEMIC accomplishments and capabilities, your letters of recommendation should provide one of the most reliable windows into your character. Here again, your letters should document and enhance what you say about yourself. They can explain the importance of any activity that takes place on campus, and sometimes off campus as well. They can provide perspective on you as a person and as a member of the school community or the organization to which you belong.

Extracurricular activities can add dimension to your application even if you don't have a recommendation commenting on them. They are a means for you to develop and demonstrate leadership, teamwork, commitment to others through service, commitment to ideas, ability to handle stress, adaptability to change, and skills like planning, budgeting, and organizing.

What kinds of activities are best for prospective law students? As with your undergraduate major, what you do for extracurricular activities does not matter as much as does the energy and enthusiasm with which you do it, and the commitment you make to it.

If you have an artistic talent or even if you just have a passion to draw, paint, play music, or act, finished products and performance can demonstrate discipline, commitment, and in some cases, teamwork. The development of discipline and teamwork skills in artistic endeavor is as important as it is in sports, and the very interest you show in these aspects of life add dimension to you as a person. Among the many talents displayed by HLS and NYU students are singing, painting, drawing, playing musical instruments, dancing, and acting, as well as athletic ability in a variety of team and solo sports.

Peter was a wonderful addition to the Annual Law School Show at NYU, where students wrote, produced, and performed a musical along with a number of faculty members. The show was a spoof on events of note during the year, as well as on faculty and fellow students. The show sported names like "Putting on the Writs," and familiar tunes had new legalese words substituted. Peter was a regular and when he started singing, the audience would gasp in amazement at his big, beautiful voice. I used to joke with him that I expected to hear him at the Metropolitan Opera someday. Indeed, he had chosen to attend NYU in order to be near his voice teacher, and was attending law school to keep his mother from worrying about him having a profession. His singing talent and experience before law school made him an attractive addition to the class. After graduating and practicing law for awhile, Peter decided to pursue his passion for singing, and a few years later, I did hear him at the Met in a number of roles, including at least once as Tamino in the Magic Flute! He also sang with La Scala, Deutsche Opera in Berlin as well as Seattle, San Francisco, and Houston Operas. More recently he has added Principal Artistic Instructor of the Young Artist Development Program at the Seattle Opera Company to his credits.

---

were a leader in more than one. The difference between high school activities and those in college is the depth to which you are expected to be involved. In college, involvement in only one or two organizations in some depth is usually more appealing than membership at a minimal level in a large number of organizations. As happens to many of my colleagues, my eyes glaze over when I see a two page list of activities. Most law schools will ask you to name the two or three activities of most interest and importance to you, and will ask that you indicate the depth of your involvement by describing your role and by indicating the number of hours spent on the activity each week. My colleague Ken Kleinrock of NYU likes to say that if the hours devoted to your activities add up to more than there are in a week, there is something wrong with the picture. And those who have an extensive list of activities often find it hard to narrow down to those that are most important because not enough time could be devoted to any one activity to rank it as important.

Venturing outside your comfort zone in your activities is as important to adding breadth to your experience in your activities as it is in your academic work. If you grew up in a privileged environment, working with disadvantaged children, at-risk teenagers, or the elderly poor will broaden your vision and add dimension to your character. If you have never had the opportunity or the resources to travel, working with immigrants or getting involved in an international student organization will add experience to your resume. An activity like this also adds to your understanding of the world and appeal to your application, to a degree it might not with an applicant who has had those opportunities and resources.

What if you have to work to support yourself or your family while you are in school? Such a responsibility may mean that you have no time for extracurricular activities. Work experience gained while you are attending school may be considered a good substitute for extracurricular experience. There are many students who are not in a position to volunteer their time because of the need to work. Admission committees make allowance for this and are often impressed by your academic accomplishment in the face of these other commitments. Whatever your work is, you can make the case that it exposes you to people and situations that broaden your perspective and enhance your understanding of the world.

YOUR RECORD OF ACCOMPLISHMENT

In absolute terms, your extracurricular activities can add to your accomplishments and skill set. Creating a product or an organization, or performing in a musical or theatrical production can provide great pleasure for you and a result that others can observe, enjoy, and evaluate. Like your academic work, your activities demonstrate skills and dimensions of your personal character, and create a record to complement your academic record.

Be sure that your claims to accomplishments and leadership roles are accurate and authentic. Exaggerated claims can lead to trouble. More than one applicant claiming to be president of a particular organization in the same year will surely raise eyebrows. You can be sure that such "coincidences" are checked out and that usually someone is not offered admission based on false claims. The number of people who claimed to be founders of a particular organization at a given school is sometimes dramatic. The reason is that everyone who joins an organization in the year in which it begins or is revived considers him or herself to be a "founder." Those who claim to be "cofounders" are generally on firmer ground, and less likely to be suspected of other puffery. In general, it is better to be understated than overstated in your claims to fame.

INTEGRATION WITH YOUR ACADEMIC RECORD

When an admissions reader examines your file, he or she is looking to understand you as a whole person. You have accomplished what your academic record shows in the context of your background and experience, and extracurricular activities are an important piece of that experience. Some activities will enhance your academic record and some will complement it. How you manage your time with both commitments will tell something about you as an emerging professional.

CHAPTER THIRTEEN

Work Experience

D OES WORK EXPERIENCE HELP you in your applications to law school? The simple answer is that work experience adds value to the degree that it is important to your experience overall. The more complicated questions are how much it helps and do some kinds of work help more than others? Does the length of time you put into work make a difference?

Work experience is another way to provide insight into your personal qualities and your character. Virtually every applicant has some paid work to show possibly including term time work, summer jobs, and/or employment after graduation. Absence of any kind of work on your resume gives pause to admissions committees.

If you are among the few with no paid work experience by the time of graduation from college, it is all the more important for you find a job and work at it for at least a year before applying to law school. Most students have summer employment, paid or unpaid. Students with financial need will also have substantial term time work. Term time work may be limited to that which is available on campus, unless you are in an urban environment and can find off-campus opportunities that are more remunerative or more interesting. Working on campus keeps you part of the academic community and convenience can be an important feature. Sometimes you can find a job that relates to your academic work, but it is difficult to find such work that pays and that you want most to do.

Summers are a great opportunity to explore fields of interest or to earn enough money to keep you in school. Those with means have more flexibility in choosing an unpaid internship or other activity that provides experience and fun in place of money. Those who must contribute to their educational expenses are more restricted; and their circumstances are understood as a demonstration of responsibility for contributing to the cost of their education.

Although each level of work can provide opportunity to show experience and skills development, employment after graduation is where you are most likely to demonstrate qualities that schools will be looking for. This is not to say that you cannot begin this demonstration in your term time work, or in your summer jobs, but the conditions for these jobs are such that you cannot count on being paid for what you want most to do.

DEGREE OF RESPONSIBILITY

Many students have to work to support themselves and their education, and admissions committees respect that need. Often that work is clerical or menial in some other way. You can find meaning and achievement in menial work, especially while you are in school. Taking pride in any work that you do, doing it to the best of your ability, and making a contribution that makes the work more pleasant, efficient, and meaningful to your fellow workers and those who follow you can make it a worthwhile experience while adding to your attractiveness as an applicant. In all your employment, you can demonstrate teamwork, discipline, adaptability to change, and respect for the work by exceeding expectations, finding new and better ways to perform your tasks, and making the job easier and more pleasant for your full-time fellow workers.

When you undertake full-time post graduation employment, you may be given more opportunity to take on real responsibility, by being entrusted with tasks that have financial consequences and where your failure to perform at a high level can cause financial losses or harm to the reputation of the organization. If you do well, you may be charged with more responsibility and higher level tasks, and given more control over your own work and that of others. The next level of responsibility includes a say in where your department or the organization as a whole is headed. At each level, more is at stake. Admissions committees like to see applicants who have been entrusted with increasing responsibility over time.

EVIDENCE OF ACHIEVEMENT

Specific achievements to which you can point in your work are another way to impress the admissions committee. If you were assigned a project you saw through from start to finish, and in which you can point to meaningful results, you may want to be sure that it is included in your application. If you have the opportunity to choose, select one where you show initiative in making good things happen, and determination and discipline in following through.

You can describe this yourself in your personal statement or in a separate paragraph describing your work experience, but another person's perspective is also valuable. This is an instance where an employer recommendation, providing documentation of the project, your contribution, and the results can add real value to your application. A description of the degree to which you consistently exceed expectations in your work, with examples included, is another good subject for an employer recommendation.

SKILLS DEVELOPMENT

Full-time employment can provide the opportunity to develop a variety of skills, including: technical, financial, analytical, writing, speaking, project and people management, and other people skills like sales, marketing, counseling, and customer service. Consider what skills you have developed in your work during school and in summers. They may help in your quest for full-time employment, and in finding full-time work that will help refine the skills you have developed and to develop others.

GROWTH OF CHARACTER

Some of the most important skills that admissions committees look for in their applicants are leadership and teamwork skills. Evidence that you have worked successfully handling complex relationships, leading or motivating others, working on teams, and accomplishing meaningful results together can add dimension to your character. If you have an interest in public service, demonstrate this by working in an organization or governmental agency that provides an opportunity for you to really experience work in the trenches. If in the course of any work you show concern for others both individually and in groups, you can demonstrate your commitment.

NATURE OF THE WORK

The nature of the work you do is not only the specific tasks of the job that you do, but also the substance with which your organization is engaged. Most admissions deans will tell you that the nature of the work that you do is not as important as how you engage with it, what skills and achievements result from your efforts, as well as growth of character and professionalism. This is definitely the case when the duration of your employment is two years or less. In fact, working in a field that appears to be entirely unrelated to law, but in which you have great interest, can make you more appealing to the admissions committee than can a mundane job that is law related.

After three years or so, the dynamic changes. The longer the duration of your employment, the more appropriate will be some connection between what you do and the law. Questions will arise, like how you explain the transition to a career in the law. Are you seeking a law degree as a natural outgrowth of the work you have been doing? Or are you looking for a change? Are you continuing a direction in which your work has taken you or are you seeking a course correction? Whatever your reasons for applying to law school after a lengthy time in another field, be prepared to provide a reasonable explanation.

Some kinds of work that lend themselves to a transition to a career in law include any kind of business experience, including computer software and hardware; work in the criminal justice system, including everything from the FBI to police work to social work; work in the health care industry; or the arts and entertainment industry.

Any work in an international context could also give rise to an interest in law. Some admissions committees particularly favor international work like the Peace Corps, or work within the United States in organizations like Teach for America or Americorps. Any of the latter would qualify as short-term employment, with the extra dimension of service, and the perspective it adds. Military service is attractive, for the service itself, but also for the discipline it develops and for the perspective it brings to the class.

RANGE AND DEPTH OF EXPERIENCE

The specific substance of the work that you do may be law related or the skills you may have developed may be directly related, collateral, or complementary to those you will need as a lawyer. For the older applicant, the evolution of your career may lead you to law or it may add a dimension to the classroom that is of value. You may have worked in a variety of areas, and your breadth, as well as your depth, of experience may be what brings you to applying, and it may be what interests the admissions committee. In either case, the level you have achieved in your previous work, and the breadth of experience and skills you bring to the class, can make a big difference in your application. By the same token, if you have bounced around in a number of dead-end jobs, or have not found success in the other areas you have tried, you may find that even strong prelaw quantitative credentials will not save you.

FINDING A MENTOR

Finding a mentor in your work is as important as finding a mentor in your academic experience. Have your antennae up for possible mentors when you seek a job, or when you are making a choice among job opportunities. If you have the good fortune to work directly for a person who shows an interest in your development and who is willing to guide you as you undertake difficult challenges, you will have also found a person who will offer you a very strong and helpful recommendation. Even if you don't work directly for someone like this, look for someone in the organization whom you can get to know and seek guidance from, without being a threat to your immediate supervisor, and who might someday serve as a recommender.

CHAPTER FOURTEEN

Personal Statement

IN THE FEW DAYS after you have taken the LSAT, you may have a moment when you breathe a sigh of relief at having completed, for better or worse, the most difficult component of your application to law school. This moment will last until you focus on the fact that you have to write a personal statement. How do you get across to the admissions committee everything about who you are and what you want to do with your life in two short pages?

The simple answer is that you cannot tell everything, even if you had ten pages, or one hundred pages. You have to make choices to write about something that tells the readers enough about who you are and where you are going without boring or irritating them. You want them to like and admire you and to hope that you will join the class that they are putting together.

Your personal statement has two main components that are of interest to the admissions committee. The first is content. You want to have the readers get to know more about you than what is contained in the rest of your application. You will have to choose what you can write about that will convey who you are and what you will add to the class. The second is execution. To get your message across, you must organize your ideas and present them in a way that grabs the reader, all the while demonstrating your ability to produce a piece of polished writing.

As you make your choice about what to write about, think about your audience. Who are they and what are they looking for? You know that they are members of the admissions committee or an admissions dean, looking for people who are smart and capable and who will add a dimension to the class they will join. You know that they already know some things about you from the questions they asked on their application form and from the letters of recommendation submitted on your behalf. They have seen your academic transcript and your resume. What more do they want and what do you want them to know? The personal statement presents a challenge and an opportunity to add a new dimension to your application.

WHAT SHOULD YOU WRITE ABOUT?

If they ask you to respond to a specific question on your application, the task seems easier. Questions might include the most obvious "why do you want to go to law school?" or "why do you want to be a lawyer?" They might ask you to describe your strengths and weaknesses, or to describe an event or activity that has been important to you. Another possibility is to describe an achievement or a failure from which you learned something valuable, or to tell about how you dealt with an ethical issue presented in your work, your academic career, or your extracurricular activities. If you are asked to answer a specific question, whatever it is, your task is made easier by the framework it provides. Find something in your personal experience that addresses the question and write a statement that answers it.

It is more likely that you will be asked an open-ended question, to tell something about yourself or your experiences that will help the readers to get to know more about you than is otherwise evident in your application. This is more difficult than finding a way to answer a specific question. Not only will the readers consider the substance and execution of your statement, but they will also evaluate your choice of what to write about.

So how do you choose your subject and decide what to say about it? Think of the personal statement as your opportunity to have an interview with each and every reader of your application. What is special about this approach is that this is an interview where you control the questions. To prepare for this hypothetical interview, examine your application for what it already conveys, and decide whether you want to introduce a new facet of yourself or elaborate on something that is already discussed in your application. The key is to limit what you say to the framework of answering the one or two questions that might come up in an interview of fifteen to thirty minutes. If you were preparing for such an interview and you could feed the questions to the interviewer, what would you have them ask you and how would you answer it?

You might choose to tell about a course from which you learned a lot, or an academic challenge you faced. Crises and turning points are always a good focus. You might talk about an artistic or cultural experience or something you encountered in your travels or study abroad. Your work and your extracurricular and community experience might also convey something important to you and something about your character.

When you examine the rest of your application, try to see what kind of a picture of you it paints. Think of your application as a puzzle that is also your portrait. Is there something that will round out your portrait, fill in a missing piece, or sharpen the focus and provide details that are critical to capturing your expression? Is there something missing, or are there some aspects that you would really like to explain in more depth? If so, you have found your subject, and now you are left with the questions that you hope will be asked. Do you want to demonstrate intellectual ability that might not come through on your transcript?

Do you want to show determination, perseverance in the face of adversity? Or do you want to show compassion and concern for others? What kinds of questions would you hope to be asked so that you can convey these qualities?

Remember that a fifteen to thirty minute interview would allow only one or two questions to be answered in depth. If there were two questions, the second might be a follow up to the first. One major goal of your personal statement is to come across as a being full of vitality, jumping off the page and into the chair across from your reader! Make the questions you ask yourself give you a chance to do that.

WHAT FORM SHOULD THE STATEMENT TAKE?

When I encourage you to think of your personal statement as an opportunity for an interview, I do not mean that it should be constructed as an interview, or written in an interview format. You want to come across as a vibrant, living and breathing human being that others will want to know, and nothing will flatten you out more than trying to use a structure or a gimmick to get yourself across. Don't let the form your personal statement takes overshadow the message you want to convey.

In the course of reading about a quarter of a million personal statements from applicants to law school, I have seen just about every gimmick, including statements written as interviews, depositions, trials where the applicant is the defendant, newspaper interviews of you as the famous lawyer, and even obituaries, where you, the deceased, have died while still serving as a Justice of the Supreme Court of the United States. Nothing will kill your chances more effectively than the obituary. Why? Because not only is it a gimmick, but also it primarily describes what you hope to do after you have graduated from law school, and very little about yourself to date. And you won't come across as a living, breathing person whom they can imagine in their class. Anyone can dream of being a Supreme Court Justice. No one else has the exact combination of background, experience, and accomplishment that you have.

MARKETING YOURSELF

Your personal statement is your principal opportunity to market yourself directly. What facets of yourself do you want to shine through? Are they really qualities that you have, or do you just wish you had them? Remember that the admissions committee wants to get to know you better than they can through the other aspects of your application. They actually want to know you just a little better; they don't need to know everything about you.

Don't tell them—show them who you are by what you write about and how you write it. Always write in the first person, and write about what you know, what you have done, or what has happened to you. When you describe something you have done or has happened to you, tell it as a story. You may be the principal protagonist, or you might choose someone who helped you or who you helped. Include what you have learned from the experience or the person. You don't have to be the hero of your story and, even if you are, try not to brag. There is a fine line between describing an achievement for the purpose of showing what is important to you or has influenced your development and bragging about it.

The same goes for complaining. If you have suffered a hardship, no one wants to hear your complaint. They want to hear how you have overcome it and how you see it as a valuable learning experience. No one wants a sourpuss or "poor me" in their class. Most admissions committees like applicants who are optimists and who know how to make lemonade out of life's lemons.

If they ask you to describe your strengths and weaknesses, include examples, choosing something you have at least partially overcome as your weakness. In describing your strengths, think about your audience and choose something that will be a positive quality for you in law school. In both cases choose qualities that are authentic to you. They should be able to confirm these qualities when they read your recommendations.

Suppose you want the committee to know you as a creative person. Your creativity might show itself in some artistic or cultural ability, it might be through performance or some other form of expression, or it might be the way in which you approach everything you do. Write about something you created, and explain how it came to be. If you took something that already existed and made it into something else, explain why and how you did it. Write about your passion for your subject and how it developed.

If you want to have the committee know that you have compassion for others, discuss some activity or work in which you have been involved to show it. Tell a story that represents what you are most proud of or that best describes the qualities you want them to know about.

If you want to convey a sense of humor, be careful. You may think you're funny, and your best friends may think you're funny, but does everyone think you're funny? And even if everyone agrees that you're funny, can you get it across on a couple of pages? Remember that the readers don't really know you, and won't necessarily put your humor in context as your nearest and dearest will do. Attempts to construct a personal statement run the risk of making you look flip or at least not a serious applicant. Sometimes a touch of wit, carefully inserted in the statement, can be very effective, but you can never tell for sure who is going to see it, or how those who do will react.

In all of these scenarios, remember that your resume should reflect at least a glimmer of what you are writing about, and that a recommender may write about it as well. If you think a recommender might comment on the same achievement or activity you have chosen, be sure to be a little understated rather than overstated in your own comments, lest the recommender minimize the accomplishment. It will cause no problem if you are a little understated and your recommender waxes ecstatic. Authenticity is key to every part of your personal statement and your own presentation of yourself. Even if they have not read the 250,000 personal statements that I and a few of my colleagues have, most admissions deans have read enough to recognize what rings true.

GETTING HELP FROM BOOKS AND THE INTERNET

The concept of authenticity brings me to an important point. It is important that your personal statement be from you, by you, and in some way about you. As you thrash around trying to think about what to write, you may succumb to the temptation to look at the books of essays that got people into Harvard Law School, or into a law school somewhere. There are similar claims made by various organizations and individuals on the Internet. Some even offer to write your statement for you or at least to rewrite it for you based on a draft you submit. There are a number of considerations you should entertain before making use of these tools.

First, you should be sure that you will not try to model your own statement on one of these, especially one that seems to be unusual. After having read even 10,000 personal statements, admissions officers have seen it all, or at least most of it, and they might even recognize the "model" you have chosen. Copying the statement wholesale, or with minor changes, may be the whole reason to deny your application. In recent years, I saw a statement that is actually famous, and was originally written by a college applicant. It begins "I leap tall buildings with a single bound" and continues to make extravagant claims of accomplishment, but ends with "but I have not yet been to college." An applicant to law school changed a few words, including changing "college" to "law school." Needless to say, this otherwise reasonable applicant bit the dust.

Second, the personal statements you are looking at on the Internet and in books are about someone else, not about you. Trying to wedge yourself into a similar format may cause you to lose the vitality that makes you jump off the page, and the authenticity that only you can bring to your own statement. Trying to emulate what someone else has written will make you look stiff and uncomfortable, and your statement will not ring true. If you want feedback on your statement, ask a relative or a friend who knows you well to read it and to tell you whether the person they know is coming through. Presumably they like you and will be able to recognize the likeable person they know as the author of the statement.

Third, you run the risk that your personal statement will look very much like others in the same applicant pool. On more than one occasion, I have found almost identical personal statements from different applicants, or at least too close to be a coincidence. This would be especially likely if you have someone write it for you or even rewrite what you have written. One of the reasons that schools read the writing sample on the LSAT is to compare the style of writing to that on the personal statement. Even accounting for differences between writing under pressure on a topic assigned, and the polished sample submitted with the application, the experienced reader can detect the degree to which you might have received help.

Fourth, even if the claims are true and the applicant who wrote the essay in the book or on the internet was admitted to the school in question, there is no assurance that he or she was admitted because of, rather than in spite of, the personal statement. So don't put too much emphasis on their claims.

PRESENTATION

After you have decided what to write about, think about presentation. Plan on working through several drafts before you have a product ready to submit. Give yourself enough time to put it aside at least for a few days before you revise it. Answer any specific questions, demonstrating that you can take an assignment and respond directly.

Organize your thoughts before you begin. You may decide to change the organization when you revise your work, but creating an outline of your ideas first will provide structure to your statement, facilitating flow and coherence. Once your outline is in place, flesh out the ideas that you want to present.

Follow directions. If you are asked to limit your statement to 500 words, or two pages, don't go over by 50 percent. Don't reduce the font size and expand the margins to fit 300 or more words onto two pages. Readers will know that you are trying to say more than was recommended. If you are going over, first consider what value your extra words will have. If you are convinced of their importance, use three pages for what you have to say. The tired eyes of the admissions reader will thank you for keeping your statement easier to read.

If you are an older applicant with extensive experience, or if you have a complex backgrounds or unusual circumstances, you might have reason to write more, or to include an additional statement. But if you do so, do it with the understanding and an acknowledgment that it is more than recommended.

Keep your statement simple and straightforward. Don't try to weave disparate subjects into one statement. You may be sending a mixed message. For example, if you feel the need to explain a bad grade or a low LSAT score, don't try to include the explanation in a statement about your achievements, even if your achievements counter the problem. Including some reference to a feature that might give the reader pause about you with a discussion of accomplishments that should make you an attractive applicant could blunt the positive effect. If you have an explanation for weak features of your file, use a separate page for addenda and limit your explanation to one or two short paragraphs.

If you can use a ten cent word instead of a ten dollar word, do it. Fancy words should only be used when they are the most appropriate choice, and nothing else will do. If the reader has to look up the word to be sure you used it correctly, you will want to be very sure you did. I have had occasion to check out words from time to time and, almost universally, the word was used incorrectly.

Avoid platitudes and clichés. If a cliché comes to mind to express what you want to say, think about whether there is another way to say it. If you want to use the cliché as a place marker for a future revision, mark it as such so that you are sure to replace it.

If one of your schools asks a specific question, and the others leave it open ended, resist the temptation to send the same statement to other schools. One year we added a second essay to our application, asking applicants to discuss their relationship to the world of ideas. Not only did we get a lot of statements that began "My relationship to the world of ideas is…" but also we drove our colleagues at other law schools, who had to read the statement in their applications, almost completely nuts. We abandoned the directed statement the following year. It may have separated out some really remarkable people who were able to respond brilliantly, but we already knew they were outstanding.

If you are responding to a specific question on one application, you can sometimes use some of the ideas, and develop them in a different direction, but don't use it intact elsewhere unless it is exactly what you want to say to every school. When you are writing an essay that is specifically tailored to one school, whether it is in answer to a specific question posed, or to make the argument that you are a perfect match for the school, be careful that the other schools to which you send it might also be a match. Above all, if you use the name of your targeted school in the statement, be sure to change the name everywhere in your statement for all other schools. There is nothing that turns an admissions dean or committee off more completely than a definitive statement about why you want more than anything to attend a rival school.

When you have finished each draft of your statement, put it aside again and look at it afresh in a few days or a week. If you haven't already done so, have a family member or friend who knows you well read it to tell you whether the person they know is coming through. Proofread it carefully, checking for spelling and grammar. Edit, edit, edit.

REVIEW WHAT YOU HAVE WRITTEN WITH THESE THOUGHTS IN MIND:

To explain "Why law?" when that question is not specifically asked, do so as a subtext. Show them why law, don't tell them.
To show your creative writing talent, particularly poetry, do so as an extra submission rather than writing your statement in iambic pentameter. That gimmick might have worked for a college application, but it won't fly for law school.
Don't repeat your entire resume in prose, let alone poetry.
Don't describe yourself as a recipe, with a cup of enthusiasm, a pinch of wit, etc.—another gimmick.
Don't complain or whine.
Don't tell them more personal detail than what your good judgment tells you is necessary to make your point. Some personal, private matters should remain just that.
Do show how you think.

Keep a focus narrow enough to allow you to go into some depth and stay within the space recommended. No full life history. No shopping lists of accomplishments.

Show signs of a lively mind.

Don't be slick. You could slide right off their list of admitted applicants.

Don't begin your statement with a quote. In particular, don't quote Shakespeare ("The first thing we do, we kill all the lawyers"), or Robert Frost ("Two roads diverged in a yellow wood...I took the one less traveled by, and that has made all the difference"). If they read that latter quote one more time, most of my colleagues will leave you there, by the side of that road.

One final word. If you want to use a quote to live by, not to include in your personal statement, let me offer you two from Shakespeare: "Brevity is the soul of wit" and "To thine own self be true." If you follow these simple concepts, your statement will be the better for it.

CHAPTER FIFTEEN

Interviews

I N THE LAW SCHOOL admissions world, interviews are the exception rather than the norm. You may wonder why law schools don't interview everyone. Medical schools and business schools use interviews much more broadly. When you applied to college, having an interview with an admissions officer or an alumnus was standard practice. So why don't law schools?

The reason that interviews are not used widely in law school admissions is based on the way the admissions process has developed. College admissions staffs are much larger per applicant than are law school admissions staffs. For example, at HLS, the admissions staff-applicant-ratio ranged from about 1:800 to 1:1000+, whereas the ratio at Harvard College was about 1:200. To build and manage an alumni network of interviewers like those used by colleges would involve significant additional staffing. The resources allocated to most law school admissions offices have traditionally not supported such efforts.

Another reason that interviews are not widely used is logistics. The cost and difficulty for applicants to get to schools not in their region presents an issue of fairness. Those with financial resources can get to the interview, those without cannot. The cost to the school to make up the difference and make the interview process widespread and fair is not one that most schools are willing to take on simply to add another dimension to the selection process. Would the schools and the applicants benefit from the introduction of an interview process? Is the cost manageable? Both answers are yes, but to date most schools have not seen fit to undertake it.

What law school interviews do exist come in two main types, the informational interview and the evaluation interview. The first results from a request made by you or an alumnus of the school who is your relative or close friend. These are courtesy interviews, granted primarily to satisfy the wishes of the requesting party. For the purposes of admission, the interviewer may only incidentally make notes for your file.

The evaluative interview is at the invitation of the school, and may come about because your file has raised some particular questions that the admissions committee wants to explore or because the school has a practice of interviewing a segment of the applicant pool, usually people whose paper credentials place them in a group about whom the outcome of the application is up for grabs. Some schools offer the opportunity for an interview for those on the wait-list, because they are looking for people who will stand out from the pack in person, or for people whose interest in the school is stronger than that of the rest.

WHO GETS INVITED TO THE INTERVIEW?

If the school interviews a lot of candidates, you may be invited to come because you are in a group from which some people will be offered admission and others will not. The wait-list interview is a classic example. In this case, the interview is critical to your admission.

Another reason that large groups of applicants are invited for an interview is that the school wants to test their genuine interest in the school and to use the interview as a targeted marketing tool for applicants they hope to attract.

You may be invited for an interview if the school has some questions about your application. Ordinarily, you will be told that, but not always. They may be trying to test whether claims made in your application are well founded or if they are exaggerated.

When a request has been made on your behalf, you may have the impression that you have been invited, but the interview is likely to be a courtesy interview. Courtesy interviews are granted at the request of prominent alumni or leaders in the community. Alumni children are the classic invitees to the courtesy interview. Sometimes a request you make or one that is made on your behalf results in an invitation to a phone interview.

DO YOU WANT AN INTERVIEW?

If you are invited for an interview, you must accept the invitation unless you are not really interested in the school. If you are not really interested in the school, postpone the interview as long as possible in hopes of being admitted elsewhere before your interview date. Another alternative is to think of it is as a live practice interview, should other opportunities arise.

If an interview will only result if you or a prominent alumnus requests it, give careful thought to whether you really want to put the effort into the project. Ask yourself if you are likely to excel in the interview situation. Are you outgoing or are you shy? Are you sometimes awkward or nervous when you meet new people? Have you ever been through a stress interview? An interview in which you perform poorly can actually harm your chances of admission.

On the other hand, if you have always done well in interviews, are comfortable with new people, and would enjoy the opportunity to interact directly with some representative of the school, then you may want to seek one.

HOW TO GET AN INTERVIEW

If you know someone who is a prominent alumnus or a prominent member of the legal community, and they have offered to help you with your application, you might ask them if they can seek a courtesy interview for you. If they are willing and they succeed, then it will be your task to turn that interview into a successful evaluative interview.

If the school offers them to anyone who requests it, you can simply call and request one for yourself. If they do not, but they do hold information sessions, plan to attend one of those and to seek out the admissions officer afterward for further discussion of questions that you have. If you have done the preparation for an interview, to be discussed below, you may be able to turn a few minutes into a valuable encounter.

WHO CONDUCTS THE INTERVIEW?

If your interview is held at the school, you will likely meet with an admissions officer or the Dean of Admissions. Occasionally a faculty member will conduct the interview. If your interviewer is the admissions dean, a faculty member, or an admissions officer, it is likely that he or she has read your file. If the interviewer is a student or an alumnus, it is less likely that he or she has seen your file.

If you are being interviewed for a special scholarship, you may be interviewed by a panel of people, including admissions officers, faculty members, judges, or other prominent members of the legal community. This may be preceded by a "soft interview" by a student, meant to relax you and at the same time warm you up.

The style of the interviewer may depend on his or her role. If the objective is to market the school, the interviewer's style is likely to be friendly and non-threatening. If there is a question about something in your application, the style might still be non-threatening, but probing, or it might be challenging or downright stress inducing.

Some interviewers who appear to be bumblers may actually be skilled interviewers with a style that puts you off your guard. You may encounter a talker or a listener; the more skilled are likely to be listeners. Whichever kind of interviewer you encounter, whatever their role in the admissions process, you must treat all as if they will have a say in the outcome of your application. Preparation is the key.

HOW TO PREPARE

Think of the interview as a performance, and your preparation as researching your role and rehearsing for the performance. Also consider what you want to accomplish and what you want to get across in the interview, and set goals and objectives for doing so. Analyze your own application to see what they might ask about. Then prioritize what you would like them to ask about, and think about how you might turn the conversation around to that.

Look especially at the accomplishments claimed in your academics, your extracurricular activities, and your work. Be sure you can back up everything you have claimed, describing how you accomplished what you did, what obstacles you encountered, what went wrong and how you handled it, why you made the decisions you did, and who else worked with you on any given project. The interview cannot possibly cover everything in your application, but you should be prepared to discuss anything the interviewer raises. Even if the interviewer asks you a hypothetical question, you can usually turn it to a discussion of your actual experience.

Have your own questions ready. Be prepared with at least three, and maybe as many as a half dozen questions, along with follow-ups depending on the answers you get. One of the worst mistakes you can make in an interview is to ask a question about something where there is an answer readily available in their admissions materials, or on their web site. Researching the school thoroughly should help you develop some very legitimate questions about something that genuinely interests you. If you can show you have done your homework, the interview is likely to go much more smoothly than if you ask a standard question about one program or other.

Another potentially serious mistake is to ask the interviewer why you should prefer their school over a rival. Although they are perfectly capable of giving you their standard answer, it and other open-ended questions make you look lazy and put the burden of the conversation on the interviewer. It is not likely to accomplish your purpose of impressing the interviewer. If your question is about a program that a rival school also has, and you have researched it fully so that you can ask in-depth questions about it, that is another matter.

The best kind of question to ask is one related to a matter of genuine interest to you and which shows you have read their materials and those of other schools to which you are applying. For example, if the school and one or more competitors have international programs that include study abroad opportunities, but the one you are talking to neither elaborates on how those opportunities work nor whether they are available to all students, it is perfectly appropriate to ask how the study abroad time is structured, supervised from the home school, what language capabilities are expected, and/or how the student demonstrates accomplishments from the time abroad. Such a question would demonstrate your interest in such programs, including both substance and academic value, as well as some knowledge of how they might play out.

As you research, familiarize yourself with current issues at the school, and check to see if any new programs are in the works. Look for aspects of the school's programs that match with your interests and achievements to date. This will enable you to come across as authentic and genuinely interested in the school.

Once you have done your research, practice with a partner. Try to get across your ideas; get your partner to ask you difficult questions about your achievements, and to explore your weaknesses. Oral preparation is good practice for thinking on your feet.

HOW TO HANDLE THE INTERVIEW

If you are granted an interview, it is likely to last anywhere from fifteen to forty-five minutes. The typical length is thirty minutes.

Dress and groom well; you don't have to wear an interview suit, business casual is fine. Take along a resume in case your interviewer has not read your file, or to leave something that will help them remember you.

Plan to arrive at the interviewer's office just a little bit early. If you arrive very early, you might walk around the campus to talk to students or to see anything that might trigger a question, like evidence of construction, signs on the bulletin board for events that are happening, or issues that are under discussion. If there is a school newspaper, pick it up and look through for ideas or issues that you might want to be prepared to ask or talk about.

Be direct. Look the interviewer in the eye when you meet and when you are answering a question. Be prepared for informal conversation at the outset, but also for a direct dive into questions or an invitation to ask your own. Be open to cues from the interviewer; follow the lead. Be respectful. Be confident but not arrogant.

Don't ramble on; give concise answers to questions. Listen carefully to the questions, and don't be afraid of a short silence as you consider your answer. Follow up on what they say and don't be afraid to go back to a subject that has been raised if you think later of how it ties into something you have been trying to get across. It will show you were listening.

Energy and enthusiasm are always helpful. Nervousness can be defused by admitting to it. Blaming others for any weakness you are asked to discuss will not help your case. Using proper grammar and etiquette and eliminating the annoying "uh," "like," and "y'know" from your vocabulary will help.

FINAL THOUGHTS

As a tool for law school admissions, the interview is still a work in progress. Consider carefully what you might have to gain and what you could lose. If you seek and are granted one, prepare yourself as if the interview will play a significant role in the decision on your application, but recognize that the impact is likely to be minimal. If you are invited to an interview, preparation is even more important, and the impact more significant.

CHAPTER SIXTEEN

Diversity and Affirmative Action

AS AN APPLICANT, YOUR main question is likely whether and how the issue of diversity affects your application. But first, let's take a look at the recent history of diversity and affirmative action and the distinction between the two. Considered by many to be a euphemism for affirmative action, diversity is actually a broader concept.

Affirmative action, defined as a means to promote access to education or employment for groups that have been traditionally underrepresented, was the name applied in the late 1960s to the effort to redress the effects of past discrimination and to promote a representative population in the school or workplace. Taking into account the adverse circumstances, historical or current, that particular groups have experienced and/or overcome when evaluating accomplishment was one facet of affirmative action. Taking affirmative steps to assure access to educational and employment opportunity for all groups was another facet.

As demand for legal education skyrocketed in the late twentieth century, arguments over affirmative action found their way into the courts. The landmark case is *The Regents of University of California v. Bakke, 438 U.S. 265 (1978)*, in which Bakke sued for admission to UC Davis Medical School, arguing that he had been passed over in favor of minority students whose numerical qualifications were lower than his. When the case was decided in 1978 by the U.S. Supreme Court, the swing vote was Justice Powell, who found the specific way that Davis carried out their admissions program to be unconstitutional, but who described diversity as an important value and stated that race was an appropriate factor to take into account when deciding whom to admit. Bakke was admitted to Davis, and schools continued to work toward access for minorities to higher education.

Powell's opinion was that affirmative action as it had come to be understood was not a viable approach to take. What opponents of affirmative action called reverse discrimination to redress the effects of past discrimination and use of quotas to ensure access to education was not permissible. Instead, schools could seek diversity in their student bodies and employees by taking race into account, among other factors, and seeking a critical mass of students from minority backgrounds. This was a way to gather the best mix of people rather than including a few potentially isolated minority individuals in an otherwise homogeneous class.

The most recent cases to come before the Supreme Court were two cases involving the University of Michigan, one of which involved admissions at the law school, which were decided in 2003: *Grutter v. Bollinger, 539 U.S. 306 (2003)*; and *Gratz v. Bollinger 539 U.S. 244 (2003)*. In the course of defending the case in favor of continuing its program as it existed before the case was brought, the results of a survey of law students at Harvard and University of Michigan Law Schools were introduced. They showed that law students at both of these schools found value in learning alongside people of different races and ethnic backgrounds. The most value was reported by students who had little or no previous experience with people from the other races or ethnicities. Although the Supreme Court found the undergraduate program's point system to be unconstitutional, the majority found the law school's "narrowly tailored use of race in admissions decisions to further the compelling interest in obtaining the educational benefits that flow from a diverse student body" constitutional, and its interest in having a "critical mass" of minority students to be a "tailored use." This affirmed Powell's opinion in *Bakke* for the foreseeable future.

Diversity in legal education always adds dimension to the group as a whole. The basis for seeking diversity in higher education is to enhance the community and the education of all those participating in the educational program. In a profession such as law, entry to the educational program is essential to entry to the profession.

Diversity in the classroom is not only an educational tool which provides students from all groups the opportunity to learn from each other, and particularly for the majority to learn from the minority, but also facilitates diversity in the profession which strengthens the social fabric of the larger community.

Diversity is manifested by background and experience, including adverse circumstances that must be overcome, and perspectives that add value to education. It adds value for the person who brings diversity to the class and to his or her classmates as well.

The many ways in which a particular student might add diversity to the classroom include geographic diversity, based in different regions of the United States, but also Americans born in or living for a significant period in another country. Students from other countries, both immigrants and foreign students, add still another dimension of geographic diversity. The diversity added by geography is not just that of location of origin, but also of the environment or milieu.

The experienced older student may have professional or other employment experience to add to more general life experience that adds value. Students from minority groups and from backgrounds which are disadvantaged from an educational and/or socioeconomic standpoint add a dimension to the education of those from more affluent, typically white backgrounds. Religious and political convictions add an element of diversity to the discussion in and out of the classroom, which has value for educational purposes and for preparation to practice a profession like law in the real-world. The academic environment is a good and relatively safe place to learn about differences and to develop understanding.

Diversity makes a contribution to the educational environment, but also to the profession and to society as a whole, by generating respect for others in the learning environment, which carries over to the professional environment and then eventually to society at large. It is a slow process, but students who are exposed, or who expose themselves to people different from themselves benefit in the whole variety of ways described above. Most people in the educational and professional environment value diversity.

WHAT DOES THIS ALL MEAN TO YOU AS AN APPLICANT AND FUTURE LAW STUDENT?

If you are a minority student, specifically from Black, Hispanic, or Native American heritage, you may be a potential student law schools are very interested in as they seek a critical mass of students from minority backgrounds, or you may at the very least add diversity to the student body.

If you are disabled, the circumstances of your disability may make you a beneficiary of special consideration. If you are an immigrant who originated in a non-English-speaking country, for whom English is a second language, you may be a beneficiary of special consideration when the admissions committee considers your LSAT.

If you have overcome adversity in your background, your achievements may mean more than those of someone who has not encountered adversity. As an example, if you come from a background of socioeconomic disadvantage, you have likely also experienced educational disadvantage. Poor educational preparation does not mean basic deficiency in ability or intelligence although it may have resulted in lower grades or scores on standardized tests. The admissions committee may decide to choose you over applicants with higher grades and scores when they consider your academic accomplishments in the context of your opportunities to achieve.

Racism still exists, and students from minority backgrounds still face hurdles in their quest for equal educational opportunity. Stereotyping and blaming the victim for his or her educational deficits still find their way into the larger community discussion. Most admissions deans and committees have, like me, observed the success of a good number of people given an opportunity through affirmative action, and are committed to assuring that there will be a critical mass of minority students in the entering classes of our law schools.

The best way I know to describe how the admissions committee looks at applicants when considering diversity and hardship overcome is what my colleague Todd Morton, formerly of Harvard and now Dean of Admissions and Financial Aid at Vanderbilt University Law School, describes as considering your achievements in the context of your opportunities to achieve. If your accomplishments are considered in this way it is possible that lower grades or scores or less exciting work experience in the face of socioeconomic or educational obstacles is actually valued higher than that of someone else with stronger grades, scores, and/or experience, who has had greater opportunity to perform and to experience more prestigious schooling and employment.

What does the quest for diversity and critical mass of students of color mean to you if you are not from a minority background, are not disabled, and have not experienced socioe-conomic or educational disadvantage?

It may mean that you will be placed on a wait-list for a school, rather than admitted. If that happens to you, you are virtually certain of being admitted to a school that is at least roughly comparable. If you find, during your first year, that being at the school where you were wait-listed is the only place you want to be in law school, you can prove to them that they made a mistake in not admitting you by being at the top of your class at the school you attend and apply as a transfer student. If you do, the likelihood is that you will be admitted and will graduate from that school. As a practical matter, most students in this situation discover that their opportunities are almost as plentiful, if not as plentiful, at the school they attend initially, and the bonds they have forged with that school keep them there.

CHAPTER SEVENTEEN

After the Admissions Decision

B Y EARLY SPRING YOU should have decisions from most of the law schools to which you have applied. At this point, you must make a decision about your first choice among those to which you have been admitted.

If you have been wait-listed by a school that you prefer, you may not be making your final choice at this time, and if you have a hard time choosing among the options you have, you may be tempted to hold more than one possibility open while you await word from the place you really want to attend. Resist this temptation if you can, because the person who takes your vacated place may vacate one at your preferred school. You may also want to consider what if anything you can do if you have been denied admission at your top choice.

The first order of business is to choose among those to which you have been admitted, then deal with those at which you have been wait-listed, and finally consider whether there is anything to be done about those from which you have been denied.

ADMISSION OFFERS

Plan to visit all the schools to which you have been admitted and are still seriously considering. Attend the Admitted Applicant Program if they have one and you can work it into your schedule.

For these programs the schools usually put together all the people to whom you could possibly want to address questions. You will meet students, administrators, faculty members, and possibly alumni. You will also meet many of your own classmates-to-be. Although not all of the people attending will end up at that school, you may end up at another school with some of them. Being there with other admitted applicants provides a good opportunity to hear what questions other students have and to share your experiences in the admissions process with those in a similar position.

Even if you are visiting on your own, with no special program, spend at least one whole day if at all possible. If you have been admitted, and are at all serious about attending, consider spending a second day, especially if your first day involves attendance at an admitted applicant program. Visiting gives you a chance to get a feel for the place and to corroborate what you have learned through written materials, your previous research, and the advice others have given you.

Assess the comfort level for you personally by talking with current students, faculty members, and administrators. Talk to more than one person when you visit a campus. Don't limit yourself to the person the admissions office has available, but you might want to talk to that person too. Bear in mind that some people may be cheerleaders while others may have an axe to grind, and that in some instances you may be learning more about them than about the school.

PEOPLE, PHYSICAL ENVIRONMENT, PROGRAMS, AND PLACEMENT

The factors that affect the decisions of admitted applicants can be divided into four categories that I call the four P's. The people with whom and from whom you learn, the location and physical environment, any programs that are distinctive to the school, and your prospects for employment after graduation are the principal deciding factors for most admitted applicants.

People

What difference does it make who your classmates are? Are you stimulated to do your best by classmates who will challenge you, or does that feel like competition and make you uncomfortable? Everyone likes cooperation, but does being laid back seem like complacency to you? Your experience in college may have provided you with some understanding of the optimum learning environment for your learning style and your needs. Do you do better as a big fish in a small pond or a small fish in a big pond? What would it be like for you to be a big fish in a big pond? A small fish in a small pond? Your classmates will be a part of your life throughout your career and you will learn from them in law school and beyond. What mix of colleagues do you want for yourself? Do you want to be around people who think the way you do? Or do you prefer to be with people who think differently?

By visiting you should get a sense of the makeup of the student body, including range in age, gender and racial diversity, geographical diversity, and differences in perspective.

What difference does the faculty make? The faculty as a whole might make a difference in choosing a particular school, particularly if teaching is emphasized. However, if you choose to attend any school because of one faculty member, be warned that faculty members do move around from school to school. Even if they do not leave your chosen school forever, they may go on sabbatical, or visit at another school for a year that might be crucial to you when you most want to take their course.

What difference do the alumni make? Strange as it may seem, since they won't be in school with you, alumni can make a difference for you both while you are in school and more so after you graduate. If the school has an alumni mentor program, and you are interested in staying in the geographic area, the alumni may be helpful in terms of future employment. Meanwhile, the advice and support they can provide while you are in school can help you with your academic planning.

Physical environment

Do the facilities, including classrooms, library, cafeteria, and other gathering places seem like a pleasant environment for study and interaction with others? What aspects of your environment made your college experience happy and what do you wish were different? As you have matured, are your needs and wishes developing and changing? Your surroundings can contribute to a pleasant working environment and facilitate your studies.

Does the school have a good central meeting place like a lounge or cafeteria, where you would be likely to bump into fellow students or faculty members? Is there a student center? Is the school located on a campus? Is the campus interwoven with the city, or walled off? How far away is the B school or any other school at which you might want to cross-register?

Are the housing options conducive to a positive learning environment? Is there housing on campus? If not, where do most graduate and professional students live? Is there plenty of opportunity for out of class contact with fellow law students and other graduate students in some of the possible living arrangements? Are there alternatives that are both affordable and secure? How will you feel coming back to it late at night?

Does it feel safe around the school? What do the school's records show about any incidents on or near campus? How porous is the campus?

Programs

In publications, on the Internet, and every other way the schools communicate with applicants, they emphasize what is special about them. This may take the form of special programs they have developed. They will present the advantages of whatever program they have. If you want to know the negatives of any particular school's program, ask someone at a competing school to critique it for you. Be subtle. This may be more complicated than you think, because most school representatives will not openly criticize another school. Present the question in a neutral and hypothetical way, and you will get a more helpful response.

For example, you can ask a school which does not feature study abroad, but does have international law as a specialty about the advantage of studying law abroad if you are interested in practicing international corporate law. They will either tell you why there is no advantage to it, or they will describe a way for you to do it even though it is not part of their program.

You should consider the response critically, because you are asking someone who might prefer you to choose their program over that at the other school. In all schools which have programs that interest you, check out the number of courses offered and the number of professors who are expert in the subject. Check to see if the courses you want are offered every year and, if not, how often they are offered.

Joint degree programs

If you are interested in a joint degree program, the quality of that program may enter into your decision to attend. Unless you are already admitted to the other school, you may have to evaluate the degree of difficulty of being admitted to the program, and how much you want to go there.

If you have been admitted, and are simply trying to decide at which school you should begin, my advice is to start at the school in which you are most interested. There is a chance that, after you have begun your classes, you will realize that you need only the one degree to do what you want after you graduate. The ability to cross-register and take a few courses at the other school may seem like enough for you.

Joint degree programs generally save you up to one year's time in school, compared to how long it would have taken to earn each degree separately.

Contrary to what many applicants think, joint degrees do not necessarily enhance placement opportunities; they just change their nature. Some of the traditional legal employers are skeptical of those who have additional degrees because they consider that the applicant is not fully committed to the practice of law. Investment banks, corporations, and government employers might be more interested in the additional education and experience than are traditional corporate law firms.

Placement

How the Career Services Offices at the different law schools operate can be a factor that makes a difference to you. There are numerous questions to consider. Is the office proactive in helping you think about career options? Are there educational programs about different career paths, help with developing resumes, training through simulation interviews, use of video to critique presentation, and the like?

How many organizations of what types interview on campus? How do you get exposure to public service if that is your choice?

What are the results? How many graduates are offered judicial clerkships, how many join large elite law firms, how many join smaller law firms? What choices do the graduates have and what choices do they make?

Some other issues to ponder after you have evaluated the four P's:

- Why did current students choose to attend?
- Was it simply that it was the "best" school they got into, or were there more varied reasons?
- What do they like best about the school, what do they think could be improved?
- What do they plan to do or hope to do when they graduate?

Consult with others, listening to what they think is important, but don't buy into misconceptions, misinformation, or incomplete information fostered by other anxious applicants in chat rooms. Taking advice from strangers on the Internet is very different from taking advice from friends that you trust.

Review your long-term goals, with the attributes of each school in mind. Continue to reassess them throughout the process.

WAIT-LIST OFFERS

If you are wait-listed at a school that you prefer over the ones to which you have been admitted, take action right away to let them know that you are still interested. If you prefer the schools to which you have been admitted over the schools that wait-list you, you have an easy task. Let them know that you no longer wish to be considered, as a courtesy to them and to those applicants on their wait-list who very much want to go there.

Don't burn any bridges by the way you tell them, even if you think they made a serious mistake by not admitting you. Your feelings and opinions could change, and you could decide to try to transfer there after your first year.

For those schools where you are still hoping for an offer of admission, consider sending a letter of recommendation from a new source and/or a letter from you bringing the school up to date on your activities and accomplishments since you filed your application. If you are still in school, send any new grades or information about new honors you have received. If you are in a job, and you have information about achievements or promotions, this is a good time to tell the school(s), and to back the information up with a letter of recommendation from your work, assuming your boss knows you are applying to law school. Stay engaged with your application throughout the summer, as long as you can still consider an offer of admission, periodically (not every day or week) checking in to reassert your interest and to let them know about any new accomplishments. Keep your options open as long as possible, and make sure your family knows how to find you if you go off on a trip just before beginning at another law school.

Eilish was on the HLS wait-list, although she was also very happy to be going to NYU.

Toward the end of the summer, she left with some friends on a trip to Europe. I called her home to offer her admission the day after her departure. Her mother knew how to reach her although it would take a few days. I agreed to hold her a place and to give her mom time to contact her. When she did, Eilish was thrown into a quandary. She had convinced herself that she would be very happy at NYU, although she had dreamed of attending Harvard. Yet she did not have time to visit HLS before making her decision. To hear her tell it, she spent the next few days of her trip pestering her friends to help her to decide where to go. It all became clear a few days after she received the offer via her mother, as she came out of St. Peter's in Rome. Not looking where she was going, she bumped into someone and knocked him down. When she picked him up and dusted him off, she saw that he was wearing a Harvard Law School T-shirt. She took this as a sign and decided to come to HLS. She turned out to be a brilliant student and a wonderful member of the community, and I am eternally grateful that the person she bumped into was not wearing an NYU T-shirt!

Do not let the fact that you are on the wait-list make you think that you are somehow inferior to those who have already been admitted, and that therefore you will likely be in the bottom of the class if you are admitted. Ever since my first year as Director of Admissions at NYU, when the last person admitted to the school later became a vice president of the student government (he ran on a platform of "mediocrity," as the last person admitted to his class) and a member of the *Law Review*, I have been delighted to see at least some of the people admitted from the wait-list do great things. Eilish was one of those who rose to the top of her class. Among others is the winner of a Pulitzer Prize, another who became first marshal of his graduating class (that's like life-president), and at least one who had been denied, then admitted from the wait-list who later became first in his class. This kind of result is not unique, and gives admissions deans confidence that the last people chosen might very well be the best!

Once you can no longer consider an offer of admission, let them know that you must withdraw from the wait-list. Again, how you handle this could be significant, if you should ever apply for transfer admission.

DENIALS

If you are denied admission from a school you very much want to attend, you may wonder if there is anything you can do about it. Every school receives significant numbers of requests for reconsideration from denied applicants. In virtually all cases, the decision remains the same, since the original decision was arrived at after a careful review of all factors. Consider taking this approach only if you have substantial positive new information to add to your file. Even with such new information, the prospects are slim. I have only seen a handful of reversed denials in all of my years in law school admissions. Each involved dramatic positive new information. All involved people where the original decision was a close case. If an applicant had been wait-listed before being denied, an example might be as simple as a dramatically improved LSAT, a really strong finish senior year, or an important award or honor. A combination of factors would most likely be required for the applicant to look different enough to change the decision. The reason it happens so rarely is that there is ordinarily not enough time for dramatic improvements to occur during one admissions cycle. Success in a reapplication in a future year is much more likely than success with a request for reconsideration.

TRANSFER POSSIBILITIES

You do have some recourse if you are denied admission at your top choice of law schools. If you perform very well at the law school you do attend, you can consider trying to transfer to your law school of choice after completing your first year. You might also consider a transfer application to schools to which you did not apply as a first year applicant, but which have risen in your estimation since your original applications. You might also have developed an interest in a particular specialization and want to attend a school where you can take a number of courses that will advance your expertise.

Factors that are most important to the decision on transfer applications are your first year performance at the school you attend during your first year and the quality of the first law school you attend. Since the LSAT is designed to predict performance your first year in law school, it is now replaced by actual performance. Your undergraduate record is still a factor, but your performance in law school is more relevant and therefore plays a bigger role.

There are advantages and disadvantages to transferring to another school. The advantages seem more evident to those who apply, and might include being unhappy with your current school. Some professional motivations include upgrading the quality of the school from which you will graduate, taking part in a special program in which you have a strong interest, or working with a particular faculty member who is preeminent in the field you want to pursue. On the personal side, being with, or at least closer to, a spouse or significant other who is tied to another city or university or to family members who are ill or going through difficult times can be motivating reasons.

Reasons that students who are sure they will try to transfer but eventually decide not to include the fact that they have bonded with their first year classmates and do not want to leave them. At the new school they will have to integrate into an already bonded community. They may discover that their job opportunities do not suffer dramatically by staying put. They are offered law review status at their original school, while at the new school they are not eligible or must enter a writing competition. There may be no financial aid grants available at the new school. Further, at some schools, pre-registration fills popular courses, and transfer students have to wait a term to be on an even footing with their new classmates.

If the plusses outweigh the minuses and you are not deterred from applying, bear in mind that there are actions you might take to facilitate your application. First, since the quality of the first law school you attend might be an important factor for some schools, you should attend the strongest school possible to begin with. Although considering your LSAT score at the point when you have first year grades to show is a violation of the Code of Good Admissions Practices, there is nothing stopping individual decision makers at the school from knowing the score and possibly being influenced by it. Schools will want to see your entire transcript of first year grades, and this may delay making a decision on your application until some time late in the summer. Be prepared to wait and to move quickly if and when the offer comes. One of my favorite students at Harvard had done really well at her initial school and was en route to another school to which she had been admitted as a transfer applicant, when we made her an offer. She just made a turn on the highway and continued on to Cambridge. She flourished at HLS and is now a faculty member at another law school, and the author of some very successful books for children.

REAPPLICATION

Like retaking the LSAT, reapplying to the same law school is usually a victory of hope over experience. Very few people who reapply are admitted the second time around. If you are thinking of reapplying to the school of your dreams rather than attending one that has offered you admission for that year, bear in mind that it may be a long shot. If you are on the wait list until the very end of the summer, you probably have a better chance than if you were denied before the wait list was made up. If it happens that competition is slightly less in the second year that you apply, you could receive a favorable answer the second time around. If your LSAT score was low for that school and you have substantial reason to believe you can do much better, that may be worth a try. If you have been offered a great job, it may be worth reapplying after gaining experience for a couple of years in the job.

FOREIGN LAW STUDY

As part of your preparation for reapplication or as an initial application strategy, you may want to consider studying law in a foreign law school. If you are especially interested in international law, it might be worth seeking admission at a foreign law school, and bringing your foreign degree into the equation of your academic record when you reapply. If the foreign school you attend is in a common law country like England, Scotland, or Australia, you could reapply and then, if admitted, request consideration for advanced standing into the second year. Even if your degree is from a civil law country, you may receive as much as a year's credit toward your electives in the second and third years.

FINAL THOUGHTS

The exercise of weighing many factors is important as you make your own choices among the alternatives you have before you. The decision will be easier if you did your homework before you applied and gave careful thought to the match between your own interests and skills and what the schools had to offer. You should continue the review and reflection process you began, but in the final analysis, it will be your instincts that will propel you in one direction or another. One issue you may consider important is financial aid, but this should not be determinative. Let's look at the question of financing your education in the next chapter.

CHAPTER EIGHTEEN

The Financial Picture

O NCE YOU HAVE BEEN admitted to law school, you face the next hurdle. How do you pay for your legal education? If you have been away from school for awhile, and are like most applicants, you may experience "sticker shock." In 2007, the average tuition nationwide at private accredited law schools was $32,367, ranging up to about $42,000.[1] Overall costs don't vary much more than 5 percent at the top private schools. In 2007, the overall student expense budget for the academic year soared over $64,000. NYU was one of the most expensive private law schools, with a budget of $64,490 in 2007. HLS was a relative bargain at an overall cost of $62,500, including tuition of $39,325.[2] Added to the layout of money is the opportunity cost of attending law school, the income you might have earned had you entered or stayed in the working world instead of devoting your time to your legal education.

You might respond to the sticker shock of private schools by considering attending a public law school, which averaged $15,455 for residents and $26,691 for nonresidents in 2007. The range of tuition is wider in the public schools, but at the top public schools the cost is close to that at the top private schools. At the University of Michigan, tuition alone for nonresidents was $41,760 in 2007, and for residents of

Michigan, it was $38,760. With $14,480 for living expenses, the overall cost was $56,240 for nonresidents and $53,240 for residents. Tuition at University of California at Berkeley seems like a bargain for residents at $26,897. For nonresidents it was $39,142, added to about $19,000 for living expenses, for a total of $45,897 to $58,142. The higher living costs make it higher cost than Michigan for nonresidents, and less than 8 percent lower than Harvard. Once the opportunity costs are added, the percentage difference diminishes further.

Financing your legal education is an investment in your future. For example, the average salary for 2005 graduates from NYU as first year associates at corporate law firms was $125,252. At Berkeley, the average salary overall was $107,000. For those entering the law school in 2008, the salary expectations for the first year out will be even higher.

To ease your anxiety about the cost of legal education, there are numerous ways to mitigate the monetary cost of your education, including working during the academic year, summer earnings, and financial aid in the form of grants and loans.

FINANCIAL AID

Because the cost of legal education seems astronomical, most applicants to law school and most law students tend to avoid trying to understand money matters until necessity requires it. Financial aid programs can postpone that necessity, but the savvy applicant, by understanding how financial aid works, can maximize its value.

If you were a typical college student receiving financial aid, to meet your need you likely received mostly grants with a small amount from loans each year. As a college grad, you might have borrowed $25,000 over the course of the four years. At law school, loans are the predominant form of financial aid. More than 80 percent of all law students receive financial aid in the form of loans; some estimates are as high as 94 percent. An average loan debt at the top schools is more than $100,000. Between 25 and 50 percent receive aid in the form of grants as well as loans. Even if you graduated from college debt free, it is likely that you will need student loans to help pay for your legal education. Since those loans will be with you for as long as thirty years after you graduate from law school, they are worth more than a little thought as you take them on.

Law schools consider the debt that their students take on to be reasonable and manageable. I asked Ken Lafler, Director of Financial Aid at Harvard Law School and one of the most knowledgeable and thoughtful financial aid experts in legal education, to provide an illustration showing why law schools have determined that a fairly high level of debt is reasonable. Weighing the costs of attending law school against the potential for a law degree to increase your earning potential over a period up to forty years working as a lawyer, he offered the following example, based on a calculator from the Motley Fool:

- You can earn $40,000 a year with a bachelor's degree.
- The full three-year cost of law school is $200,000.
- You can earn $25,000 each summer while in law school.
- You can earn $100,000 upon graduation from law school.
- Your current age is 22 and you will retire at age 65.
- Your annual increase in earnings, with or without the law degree, is 3% (in fact, with the law degree, your annual earnings are likely to increase at a higher rate than without a law degree).

Given these assumptions, you will "break even" on the cost of your law school education by the age of thirty, in terms of the higher income you are earning with a law degree versus the total cost of education. Over the entire term of your career with a law degree, you will earn approximately $8 million, versus total career earnings of $3.6 million with just a bachelor's degree.

You can do your own scenario using a calculator called "What is value of higher education?" on the Motley Fool web site at http://www.fool.com/calcs/calculators.htm.

If the cost of your education worries you, try some scenarios like that laid out by Ken to understand student financial aid programs at both the federal and school level. If you received financial aid as an undergraduate, the federal application forms and rules will be familiar to you, but there are some differences to consider.

Study the policies at the schools you are considering, particularly at the school you decide to attend. Understanding how the programs work will help you maximize the value of the money you have, the money you earn, and the money you borrow. Financial aid is complicated, but as a lawyer you will need to understand many complicated subjects and issues, and you might as well begin with this. The payoff in your personal financial situation could be great.

At both HLS and NYU, as well as at some other law schools, the financial aid office has been renamed the Office of Student Financial Services, because they do much more than simply deliver financial aid in the form of grants and loans. Two valuable offerings are personal counseling and group educational programs on making your own best decisions about your financial resources. You will be wise to take advantage of any such programs at your school.

File your forms early, especially while you are an applicant. Your FAFSA (Free Application for Federal Student Aid) application, available at http://www.fafsa.ed.gov, should come first. Check the deadlines for admitted applicants at the schools to which you are applying. Some schools send their own forms to new admits, requesting information to help them evaluate your financial need. To facilitate your eligibility for need-based aid, file your own income taxes early and encourage your parents strongly to file theirs early. You and your parents should be prepared with current bank statements, mortgage information, medical payments, business financial statements, stocks, bonds, IRAs and other retirement accounts, your credit history, and any current loan information including student loans. The financial aid you may receive comes in various types, ranging from that based on need, or your family's financial situation, to that based purely on your own academic merit or other demonstrated qualities. Let's look at the various ways that financial aid is determined and distributed.

Need-based aid

Need-based aid is money designed to meet the shortfall between your resources and those of your parents and the budget set by the school, which includes tuition, fees, living expenses, books, and the like. The money is distributed to you in the form of grants and loans.

The resources to meet the school's budget include your assets, those of your parents, scholarships including outside scholarships, loans, income from working during the year, and savings from summer work. If your scholarships, loans, and work/study resources exceed the budget, the school must reduce either your grant or your loans in order to meet federal regulations.

To determine your eligibility for need-based aid, financial aid officers use a national standardized set of need analysis guidelines to measure your family's financial strength and ability to contribute to the cost of your education. If you receive any federal loans, the school must comply with federal regulations with respect to financial aid.

The evaluation of your family assets involves analysis of financial information supplied by you and your parents. The calculation of the contribution expected from you and your parents takes into consideration a variety of factors, including the age of your parents, family size, the number of family members in college or graduate school, the cost of living in your home region, equity in your home, savings and other assets, and your parents' current income potential. Your own savings and other assets are also taken into account, as is your summer income and expenses.

Sometimes special circumstances require professional judgment on the part of the financial aid office. Professional judgment is the latitude given to financial aid professionals, under federal student aid methodology and within schools' institutional policies, to override or adjust the standard needs analysis formula based on special circumstances.

Need-based aid works like this: once your family contribution has been calculated, it is subtracted from the overall cost of attendance (the student budget) to arrive at "financial need." This is the amount that the school estimates must be provided in financial aid resources to meet the total cost of attendance after the family contribution. Typically, you will be expected to borrow an amount of money before you are eligible for grants. At many schools, this is called the "base loan" or "unit loan" threshold. If the school has need-based grants and meets full need, any remaining need above that required borrowing threshold is what you will be offered as a need-based grant. You are typically free to borrow beyond the base loan threshold to make up the contribution imputed from your parents, if your parents are not actually helping you financially. This borrowing will generally be through private loan programs, which typically require that you demonstrate a good credit record or arrange for a creditworthy cosigner.

For example, suppose the budget for a year at law school is $60,000. After considering your parents' information, the school determines that they can contribute $15,000 to the cost of your education. You are expected to contribute $2,500 from your summer earnings before you enter. Your family contribution is $17,500. Subtracted from the overall budget of $60,000, your need is calculated at $42,500. The base loan required by the school for all students is $22,500. You can get federal Stafford loans amounting to $18,500, and borrow an additional $4,000 from one of the private lenders recommended by the school. The school in this example also has a self-help component of $5,000, which you can meet by working, winning an outside scholarship, or more borrowing from the private lenders. Your loans and your self-help add up to $27,500, which is subtracted from your need of $42,500. Your scholarship grant in this case will be $15,000.

Merit scholarships

Merit scholarships are used by most schools to "enrich the class" by attracting some top applicants who might, absent the financial aid differential, choose to attend a competing school with stronger appeal. Most merit scholarship decisions are made by admissions committees or some special faculty committee. Sometimes merit scholarships have an educational or programmatic component that sets the winners apart from the rest of the class.

For many years, NYU has offered the Root-Tilden Scholarship to admitted applicants who have demonstrated capacity for and commitment to public service. This program provides not only money, but also special educational and public service opportunities including summer internships.

As of 2007, twenty-one schools have followed suit with formal programs, and thirty-four have public interest scholarships. Two more schools have both kinds of programs.[3]

A different model of merit scholarship is the Dean's Fellowship at NYU, where the winners are invited to become members of colloquia with faculty members and participants in other special academic programs and activities. Many schools have academic merit scholarships; some are along the lines of the NYU model and others have no other benefit than discounted tuition for candidates according to how attractive they are to the school.

If you expect to apply for one of the programmed merit scholarships, investigate each program to understand the requirements. It might be important to apply when you first file your application. You might be asked to file a formal application and write a special essay, or you might simply be asked to check a box indicating your interest. Some schools will invite you to apply for special programs after you have been admitted, others might offer you the scholarship with no expression of interest on your part.

The likelihood is that if you are a strong candidate for admission to a top law school, you will be offered a merit scholarship at numerous less competitive law schools.

Accepting a merit award typically means accepting a place in a law school at least one notch below the strongest school to which you are admitted. There are a few exceptions to this. If you possess a special talent or expertise that is of particular interest to an individual school or group of schools, you might find that your top choice is interested in giving you a merit scholarship.

For example, candidates with a science, technical, or computer background have been in demand by employers, and schools with expertise in intellectual property or patent law have reached out for the best applicants. Do your homework. Knowing which schools have interests that mesh with your expertise and interests might help you win a scholarship without sacrificing your choice of schools.

If the merit scholarship approach is attractive to you, and you want to maximize your options, do not plan to apply to early decision programs. Early decision programs require that you accept the offer of admission that is made during the time period designated by the program. If you are admitted early decision to a school, you become a "hostage," no longer free to negotiate whether or not you will attend based on the quality of your financial aid offer. Merit scholarships are ordinarily no longer on the table.

Early action programs are different, in that you still have the option to accept an offer from another school. Thus, you are still in the mix when decisions are made about merit scholarships.

If you request and are granted deferred admission at your school of choice, you will likely be required to sign an agreement that you will not apply to any other law schools, without first obtaining the permission of the law school from which you are deferred. This commits you to attendance at this law school, and usually takes you out of the pool for merit-based aid.

However, if you receive a financial aid award decision before you request deferred admission, you may have some bargaining power. If you are offered a merit scholarship, you may even be able to secure that scholarship for the future year.

Even need-based schools may offer you a different amount if your financial circumstances change over the course of your deferral. This is especially likely if you are working to help pay for law school. What you manage to save could reduce the amount of need-based grant you are offered.

Merit scholarships constitute a zero-sum game for most law schools, with bidding wars for the strongest students. Because so many schools are in the "game," each gains a few strong students and each loses students lower on their list to schools that offer them a merit scholarship. Millions of dollars are diverted from needy students, often landing in the hands of those who don't demonstrate financial need.

If you win a merit scholarship, consider your choices carefully before you give up attending a stronger school in favor of having a smaller loan debt burden when you graduate. This choice could result in fewer or less remunerative opportunities when you graduate. If this happens, you might have been penny-wise and pound-foolish in the choice you have made. That said, if you are offered a merit scholarship at your top choice of schools, there is no reason not to take advantage of it.

Merit packaging

Merit packaging is a modified version of the merit scholarship, mixing need with merit. The school meets the need of the applicant with a combination of scholarships and loans. The mix of grants and loans is influenced by how attractive the candidate is to the school. For example, consider a school that ranks its admitted applicants into groups A, B, and C. Translated, that means A: the most desirable, B: desirable, and C: "fungible." The most desirable would be a merit scholarship candidate at the school who also has demonstrated need for financial assistance. The fungible candidate can be easily replaced by almost equally attractive candidates on the waitlist, and will get no merit aid. The B candidate is attractive and the school has figured that it is worth X amount to try to get him or her to choose to attend. If all the A candidates turn the school down, some B candidates will become A's, especially if they have not yet made a commitment to attend.

In the world of merit scholarships and merit packaging, negotiation is common between admitted applicants and schools. The schools may not like to negotiate, but they usually prefer it to losing a desirable candidate.

Some schools are very upfront about what they will do: for example, the University of Texas has a financial aid matching program where they offer merit money to admitted students who have received financial aid packages from selected law schools. The "selected" law schools are those to which Texas is most likely to lose admitted applicants, and the amount of money involved is designed to make the cost of attendance at UT equal to or less than that at the competing school. Texas can afford to do this, because they have very low tuition for in-state students, and not that many out of state students.

Other schools have similar approaches to that of Texas; they just do not announce it on their web site. If you have received a very generous offer from one school, but prefer another, you can try negotiating with that school. You may not succeed, but if you approach it openly and reasonably, no harm is done.

The best way to negotiate is to send a copy of the merit award letter to the school you hope will match it. Do not bluff about it. If you describe the offer exaggerating the amount and do not send documentation, your bluff could be called and, even if you decide in the end to attend that school, you might have lost some trust at the school and jeopardized relationships that will last your entire three years.

If the school does not negotiate, or if they are unwilling to meet the other offer, you can decide how important the money is to you, and how much you want to attend the school. On the other hand, sometimes even a school which does not negotiate is willing to take another look, especially if the other offer is need-based. Financial Aid officers frequently use professional judgment to evaluate need. There is room for disparate judgments over such issues as parental retirement accounts, the value of a small business, or the estimated equity in a home.

Outside scholarships

The best kinds of merit scholarships to win are those offered by organizations outside the school. Outside grants don't take money from needy students at your school. They are portable and, in many cases, do not reduce your eligibility for need-based grants, reducing your loan burden rather than your grant. If you win one of these scholarships, check each school's policy on outside scholarships. Some schools will reduce your grant dollar for dollar; others will reduce your loan burden. Remember that the schools cannot increase your overall budget when you are receiving federal monies.

Outside scholarships commonly won by prospective law students are the Truman Scholarship, the Paul and Daisy Soros Fellowships for New Americans, American Trial Lawyers Association fellowships, American Association of University

Women's Education Foundation scholarships, Jack Kent Cooke Foundation scholarships, the Harry A Blackmun scholarship, the ABA Legal Opportunity Scholarships Fund, Herbert Lehman Education Fund Scholarships, Mexican American Legal Defense and Education Fund scholarships, and Congressional Hispanic Caucus scholarships.

Scholarships are also offered by county bar associations, local alumni groups, and other organizations with special interests. Many of these grants are targeted to minority students. Some law firms offer scholarship aid contingent on your accepting employment with the firm when you graduate. If you are a veteran of the military you are eligible for Veteran's educational benefits through the GI Bill. Check the web site at www.gibill.va.gov/GI_Bill_info/benefits.htm for the latest update and payment amounts for your length and type of service. If you have served in AmeriCorps, after one year of full-time service, you are eligible for the Segal AmeriCorps Education award, which in 2007 was $4,725, prorated for part-time, which can be used to repay student loans or to pay educational expenses. See the web site at www.americorps.gov for details.

If you get on the web to search for outside scholarships to help you with your legal education, beware of scholarship search scams. If you see offers that purport to help you match up with special scholarships, and they ask you for a credit card payment of any sort, do not bite. You could find that they will take your money and you will hear nothing further from them. See the Motley Fool's financial advising web site at www.fool.com/personal-finance/saving/index.aspx for an article titled "Don't get swindled by scholarship scams."

Financial independence — your family's contribution

Your parents may have told you that they would pay for college, but you are on your own for graduate or professional school. Many parents feel their responsibility for your education stops with your bachelor's degree. They may have other children to educate. If you are the last of their children, they may have begun thinking about saving for their own retirement.

From a financial aid perspective, independence from your family means that their resources are not considered when a needs analysis is conducted for purposes of determining your eligibility for need-based aid. The federal government treats you as independent of your parents once you are in graduate school, and makes you eligible for federal loans unless you have significant amounts of your own financial assets.

Unfortunately, declaring independence from your parents with respect to law school grants is not so easy, since the law schools cannot afford to step in for your parents when they choose not to support you financially while you are in law school.

Typically, law schools do not treat you as financially independent of your parents. Some schools never consider you independent for the purpose of eligibility for institutional need-based funds, regardless of how old you are or how old your parents are. Others do make you eligible, under certain conditions, which might include age or marital status.

A few schools consider you partially independent in certain circumstances, requiring only a percentage of the parental contribution calculated by the needs analysis computation. Check the policy of each school you are considering to see how they treat independence. They are working with their own institutional funds and trying to allocate them fairly. If every student were treated as independent, the most needy would be in worse straits than under a system where parental ability to contribute is taken into account.

If your parents can afford to help you, but you are truly estranged from them, or even from one parent, be prepared to document this with tax returns of your own or records from the parent who has most recently claimed you as a dependent.

Most parents, even those not providing financial support, do support you in every other way, and are willing to provide all the information that the school requests in order to make a fair assessment of your family financial strength. However, there are parents who regard the request for information as an invasion of privacy. If your parents are inclined in this direction, let them know that whatever information they provide is strictly confidential to the financial aid office, and that it will never be transmitted to anyone else, including you, without their permission. Their information can only help you with respect to your receiving need-based aid. The absence of information forces the financial aid office to impute that your parents are fully capable of supporting you, and you will be ineligible for need-based aid.

Although most schools follow the same standardized institutional methodology, based on federal methodology, to determine whether you are eligible for need-based grants, individual schools will take different approaches to your parents' assets, particularly with respect to the estimate of home equity, IRAs, Tax Deferred Annuities and other retirement assets, and with small businesses and farms. Most schools are responsive to family financial emergencies like loss of job or unexpected or extraordinary medical expenses and the like, but each school might treat them differently.

The good news is that if your parents have enough money to fully support you, but have declined to do so, you can borrow money from a variety of sources to replace their imputed contribution. As a prospective law student, provided you have good credit, you are in a good position to choose among lenders.

Credit worthiness

Good credit is important to your ability to borrow or at least to the terms of any loan you want to take out. If your credit is not good, you may have a more limited set of loan options and might need to find a credit-worthy co-signer for your loans.

You might think you have good credit and do not have to worry about such issues, but it is a good idea to check your credit to be sure and to be fully prepared for the borrowing you will do for law school.

Each year, you can obtain a free credit report from each of the major credit data agencies. They are Equifax, Transunion, and Experian. You can request the report at www.AnnualCreditReport.com. When you get your report, if you find some negative information about your credit, take immediate action to correct that information. If it is not an error, and you have already been admitted to a law school when you learn this, you can enlist the aid of the financial aid office to help clear your credit. The most common problem for recent college graduates is a credit card missed payment or disputed charge, and you can work with the credit card company to rectify the problem.

If this has happened to you, you are not alone. When you were in college you likely had your first experience with credit; college students are barraged with invitations to have their own credit card and offers that sound wonderful if they just sign up. Maintaining spending discipline is a real problem for some young people, and the best advice is to avoid using a credit card to buy anything more than you can pay back in the coming month. Pay as you go, and don't live beyond your budget. Having a credit card can help with temporary cash flow shortages. For example, HLS students would use them to book airline tickets, buy books, and pay moving expenses in advance of receiving their financial aid disbursements each year. If you know you will be reimbursed immediately, it can be perfectly appropriate to use a credit card for a relevant purchase.

It is also possible that a joint card with your parents had a missed payment or dispute, and that reflects on you as well as them. The most important problem to avoid is defaulting on your college loans, which will make you ineligible for federal loans for law school. If you do have this problem, get busy immediately rectifying the situation. The federal loan program will work with you to get you back in good standing, but it takes time.

Loans

Financial assistance for students attending law school differs from that provided for college students in that loans constitute a higher proportion of the package than they did in college. It is likely that your loan debt burden from college does not exceed $25,000, whereas your loan debt burden from law school, if you are an average borrower, will be close to $100,000. On the plus side, graduation from law school results in a much higher salary generally than did graduation from college. Also on the plus side, loans are readily available to those law students whose credit history is clear.

Federal loans are the most commonly used, and have the best terms. As long as you are an American citizen, or a permanent resident of the United States, you are eligible for the federal loan program. Federal loans are the most readily available of all loans and generally have the best terms. For graduate and professional school students, they include the Perkins loan, Stafford loans, and PLUS loans.

Perkins loans are intended for needy students and schools are provided with an allocation to administer. The university determines how much money goes to each individual unit. The most any one graduate student can receive in a year is $6,000. The interest rate is 5 percent, and interest does not accrue while you are in school.

The Stafford loan comes in two forms: subsidized and unsubsidized. The subsidized loans have a maximum of $8,500 per year. They are subsidized in that interest does not accrue while you are in school, or in deferment of loans, and you do not have to begin to repay the loan until you have been out of school for six months. Unsubsidized Stafford loans are available for up to $12,000 per year. Interest begins to accrue as soon as the loan is disbursed to you. Repayment does not begin until you have been out of school for six months. There are many options for repayment and you can repay over as much as twenty-five years if you have borrowed over $30,000. The maximum you can borrow for your entire education from the Stafford loan program is $138,500, of which no more than $65,500 can be subsidized loans, including the undergraduate loans you took out for college education. The interest on Stafford loans was 6.8 percent in 2007, and will go no higher than 8.25 percent. Some helpful web sites to learn more about student loans are the following:

www.staffordloan.com

www.nasfaa.org

www.studentaid.ed.gov

www.FederalStudentAid.ed.gov.

It is now possible for you to borrow from the PLUS (Parental Loans for Undergraduate Students) program under the same conditions as offered to your parents when you were in undergraduate school. The interest rate is higher than that of the Stafford loans, but it is a source of additional money. The Graduate PLUS program carries the same terms for cancellation on death or disability as do the Perkins and the Staffords. They also have broader deferment options than do private loans.

Other governmental loans include state financed programs like that of the Massachusetts Educational Financing Authority (MEFA), which has excellent terms for its loans. Check your home state and the state in which your school resides to see if there are special provisions that would make such loans more desirable than private loans.

Private loans are provided by a number of sources for law students to supplement the federal loan programs. Private lenders include the Access Group, a nonprofit organization founded by the Law School Admissions Council to provide loans to law students but now also provide loans to students from other graduate and professional schools. In combination with the federal loans, you can borrow a total up to the budget set by your school for your education.

Other private loan organizations are affiliated with banks, such as Citibank or Bank of America. You might also have access to a credit union or to a nongovernmental lending agency. Check with the financial aid office at your school to see if they have arranged especially favorable terms with any particular organization. Recent revelations that some schools may have designated preferred lenders based on special gifts to financial aid administrators make comparing terms offered by different lenders all the more critical.

When you choose a loan, there are a number of factors you should consider, such as which programs assess fees; the terms of the loan; your own credit history; whether you are a U.S. citizen; repayment terms, including repayment incentives or consolidation; and the like. Study the terms of each loan and decide which program fits your personal circumstances the best.

Loan forgiveness and loan repayment assistance

Loan forgiveness programs and Loan Repayment Assistance programs (LRAPs) are a significant component of financial aid programs at many law schools. LRAPs are designed to allow graduates to maximize career options and to relieve debt burden for those who undertake public service work. They come under many names and the programs vary widely, from those that supply you with additional loans to help you repay your law school loans to those that will forgive those loans over the period of years that you would otherwise be making payments.

These programs are particularly prevalent at law schools, as compared to other graduate and professional schools. Check to see if your school has such a program, and how the program works. At only two schools, Harvard and Yale, are the programs income related without reference to whether the position meets public interest definitions. These provide a safety net for those students who are risk averse to taking out large loans to finance their educations. All others expect that students will enter public service work and most require that you stay in a job for a certain number of years or plan to repay the assistance the LRAP has provided.

When evaluating your financial aid package, be sure to consider LRAPs as a part of that package. You may find that the terms of the LRAP are such that they more than equal a full tuition scholarship. The more loans you need to take out, the more likely this is to be the case.

According to a survey conducted by Equal Justice Works (www.equaljusticeworks.org, formerly known as the National Association for Public Interest Law—NAPIL)[4] there were one hundred law schools with LRAP programs, either on their own or in connection with their state LRAP (see below for state programs). This compares favorably with the forty-seven programs reported in 2000. From the school's point of view, loan forgiveness programs are a good way to stretch financial aid dollars, since only a small proportion of students go into public service work and therefore need the program. They also provide students with reassurance that they can afford to take a lower-paid public service position even if they have taken out large loans and have a high debt burden. It is another form of need-based aid, in that those graduates who undertake lower-paying jobs demonstrate need after graduation.

Since a much higher percentage of the class considers going into public service when they enter law school than actually do so after graduation, this is a much less expensive "shotgun" marketing approach than the "rifle shot" merit scholarship/merit packaging approach. It also gives the school the moral high ground for willingness to fund public service.

LRAPs are also beginning to appear as state-funded programs. As of 2007, fifteen states and the District of Columbia had them, including Arizona, Florida, Indiana,

Kentucky, Maine, Maryland, Minnesota, Missouri, Montana, New Hampshire, New Mexico, New York, North Carolina, Texas, and Washington. By far, Kentucky has dispensed the most money—$1.2 million in 2006, to forty-four participants. The other programs are much more modest. The ABA has created a resource guide for states wishing to establish them, and is encouraging states to do so. From the state's perspective, such programs can bridge the gap for lawyers working in its state agencies and organizations, but whose loan debt would otherwise preclude their working at such low salaries. Typically, the state programs are limited to work in certain agencies, and only within their own state. If you are interested in this kind of work after graduation, check to see if your state has implemented such a program.

A very small number of public service employers provide loan repayment assistance to their lawyer employees. According to Equal Justice Works, the National Association of Law Placement (NALP) conducted a survey of 4,500 employers and, from 430 respondents, found that 39 offered LRAP to attorney employees. Twenty-eight of these organizations were civil legal services organizations.[5] The highest award was for $12,000. The federal government also provides LRAP assistance to employees including, but not limited to, lawyers.

According to the Equal Justice Project, another survey by NALP showed that respondents differed about how important loan repayment assistance was, with those in the private sector rating it low, and those in the public sector rating it important, but not the most important reason for their choice of work. It is logical that those in the private sector would rate it low, since virtually no one would benefit from it. That it is important, but not most important, for those who go into public service work is also logical, since those who were not committed to public service would be more likely to enter the higher paying private sector and those committed to public service are making it a career choice regardless of money. The help provided by loan forgiveness is important, but they would find a way to undertake the work even if no loan assistance were available.

By the time you graduate, it is likely that more states will have implemented LRAPs, and since work is proceeding at the federal level, there is hope for a national LRAP for those in federal government and possibly some nonprofit work.

Working during the academic year

Working while you are in law school is a way to help your financial situation. Most schools offering need-based packages will calculate a family contribution (what you and your parents are expected to contribute to your educational expenses), sometimes separated into a parental contribution and a student contribution. However they do it, you are typically encouraged to work and/or to take out loans to provide the amount of money expected. Schools adhere to the ABA guideline that students not work during their first year of law school. This is good practical advice to help you make the best academic adjustment and therefore the most of your legal education. If you choose to ignore the advice and decide to work, at least try to find something compatible with or complementary to your studies.

After the first year, working will help ease your debt burden at graduation. Whatever work you undertake to help yourself during the academic year, check to see what your financial aid office's policy is with respect to working more hours than they recommend to you in your award letter. If their policy is to reduce loans, you can work as many hours as you want, as long as you don't exceed the ABA guidelines of less than twenty hours per week for full-time law students.

Sometimes your financial aid package will include Federal Work Study funds to help pay you to work on campus, or off campus in a nonprofit or government organization. These funds provide matching money for what the employers pay. You can work for them for a small amount of money, and you receive a competitive salary.

One of the best opportunities on campus is work as a research assistant to a faculty member. It is remunerative and provides an opportunity to get to know a faculty member and to add to your knowledge of the law. On a more general basis, your library might hire research assistants to do short-term work for various faculty members. You get to know a number of faculty members a little, and learn something about a variety of subjects.

A more social alternative is to work as a resident assistant, either at the law school or at the college, if your law school is affiliated with a university. This can be an emotionally demanding position, since you may be called upon to deal with some difficult situations involving undergraduates or your fellow law students. At the same time, it can be very rewarding if you thrive on personal interactions.

Somewhere between these two positions is to serve as a tutor, helping undergraduates with their studies or first year law students experiencing difficulty adjusting to law school classes. College faculty members might hire you as a teaching fellow in their courses in the college. Typically, professors with courses in political science, government, or philosophy find law students to be good teaching fellows. If you majored in one of these, your chance of being selected is good. If you majored in something else, you could see if that department needs teaching fellows. This kind of work is good if you like to be around undergraduates. You might also find work with the prelaw adviser or career counseling office in the college or with some other administrative or academic unit in the college or law school.

A less glamorous employment opportunity on campus might include working as a security person in the library or a dorm.

When things are quiet, you can read or study on the job. Similarly, working in the campus cafeteria might mean free meals as well as income.

Off campus work usually involves some inconvenience, including travel time, but some opportunities are worth the effort. You might find an opportunity with a local nonprofit or law firm, with the opportunity to enhance your knowledge and skills. If you were involved in debate in college, look for an opportunity at your college or another nearby, or at a local high school. The security guard gig might work in a local business. Personal service like babysitting, shopping for shut-ins, dog-walking, cat feeding and the like are choices you might make because you enjoy animals or children, or you enjoy helping others, but need to earn money while doing so. I know some entrepreneurial types who loved dogs and walked numbers of them together for good remuneration.

The key here is that you need to be available every work day or to have a reliable substitute or partner. Some more flexible options I have seen have been students who served as restaurant evaluators (great for going out to dinner for free, and earning money to boot!) and secret shoppers. These are not necessarily enough to constitute a steady job, but can add a bit of variety to life, while adding a little to your coffers.

Summer earnings and summer public interest grants

A recent study by NALP[6] surveyed a national sample of 3,905 new graduates in 2002. The respondents indicated that they covered 17 percent of their law school education with money from employment. Summer employment makes up most of this contribution, and most of this comes from the second summer, where many students are employed and the salaries approach the salaries for first year associates. The summer salaries for those working in firms in 2006 were $2,000 per week for first summer, and $1,950 per week for the second summer.[7] An explanation for the higher average for first summer than second is that a higher percentage of the firms reporting were the largest, and highest paying firms, and the students they hired for the first summer were those most in demand and/or the most experienced in their classes, and mostly from the top schools.

The fact that about 60 percent of the first year class at HLS receives Summer Public Interest Grants is emblematic of the contrast between first and second summer earnings. This contrast is common to the top law schools.

How your law school evaluates summer earnings when determining your financial aid award may influence your decision as to how hard you want to work to make a substantial amount of money during your summers. Some schools grant three year scholarships before you enter. If your school does this, you have an incentive to earn and save as much as possible during the summer so as to reduce the amount of loan you need. However, if your school assesses summer savings based on your earnings for the summer, you do not have an incentive to earn as much as you can. Some schools will create incentives by imputing savings based on your weekly salary and a number of weeks worked. If you work more weeks, they don't reduce your grant, but allow you to take out less in loans. If you work fewer than the imputed number of weeks, they still expect summer savings based on the number of weeks you would be expected to work.

Most of the top law schools, and numerous others, offer summer public interest grants to those students who want to try working in the public interest sector. HLS and NYU both offer such grants to any student who wants one, as long as they have found a suitable position. Students can work as volunteers because of the availability of the grants. They can live on the grant, and no summer savings is expected by the financial aid office.

LONG-TERM IMPLICATIONS OF FINANCING LAW SCHOOL

Your legal education is an investment of money and time, where the expected return is a highly paid job that is interesting and fulfilling, with room for growth in responsibility and remuneration. Although the costs may be somewhat mind-boggling to the average graduating senior in college, they are in line with the salary expectations on graduation from law school.

What is important for you to ponder is how to gain the best value for your money and time, given what you hope to do in your career. The top schools are expensive, but the financial payoff is more certain and more immediate.

My own view is that you get what you pay for, in terms of both money and effort. Look for good value for your own circumstances, but be wary of a penny-wise, pound-foolish choice.

With respect to what your borrowing will look like after you have graduated and begun work, there are no guarantees, but past experience indicates that even very minimal inflation will make the debt seem smaller than you first thought. Rising salaries also mitigate the consequences of debt.

Learning to budget your money will be valuable to you in law school and throughout your lifetime. It is an important life skill, like managing your time, and requires the same kind of planning and skills. Many law schools offer a financial life skills program to help students develop basic budgeting, debt management, and financial planning skills. If your school does this, take advantage of it.

Just as you need to decide how to allocate your time and set priorities, you also need to decide how you want to allocate your money, setting priorities. In both cases, some priorities are set for you. Your class schedule is set, your tuition and fees must be paid. You will also make optional choices with your money, just as you do with your time. Take control of your money, just as you do of your time. Remember that if you live like a lawyer when you are a student, you may have to live like a student when you are a lawyer. A few people manage otherwise, but your best approach will be to live like a student while you are a student, so that you can live like a lawyer when you are a lawyer. If you can manage to live frugally both as a student and as a new lawyer, you may be able to be free of student loans sooner than you expect.

If you have learned how to manage your budget while you are in law school, you will find it easier to manage your debt burden after you graduate. Up to $2,500 of your debt will be tax deductible if you make less than $65,000 modified adjusted gross income as a single taxpayer or $135,000 as a joint tax return filer. LRAPs may add to your income and put you out of contention for this deduction, but they also can mean that if you can live on the salary you make, you will receive enough assistance from your school or state to repay your loans.

CHAPTER NINETEEN

Finding Your Match in the Legal Profession

L AW SCHOOL IS A professional school, and the ultimate reason for getting into law school is to prepare for a career in the legal profession. Just as there are many roads *to* law school, so are there many roads leading *from* law school. In the course of your working life, you are likely to experience more than one of the many different venues for spending a career in the law.

Private firm practice is the most common venue, from the large elite law firms to small town practice or even hanging out your own shingle. There are also small boutique firms in specialty practice or serving public interest goals. There are a myriad of government jobs at federal, state, and local levels, including regulatory, prosecutorial, and public defender positions. Within organizations are opportunities for in-house corporate jobs and work in nonprofit or nongovernmental organizations.

The process of finding a job that best fits your personality and skills and provides you with most or all of your career related needs and desires is one that will likely occupy your thoughts before, during, and after law school. You will want to explore many varied possibilities, learn more about yourself, and experiment with different techniques to find what best suits you. In most law schools, especially those at the top of the pecking order, the career services office is there to help you with your exploration, but it will be your job to take advantage of what programs or services they offer.

Most schools offer career-related panel discussions (often using their own alumni as panelists), presentations, and workshops. For example, HLS offers a series of panels called The World of Law, each highlighting an area of practice, and an overview of the career path or paths to get into the area. Sampling the areas that interest you is a helpful way to understand them. This can be done through volunteer or paid work during the school year, and during the summer.

Drilling down to the more individualized level, most schools offer self-assessment tools and individual advising to help students to develop personalized career strategies. Resume and cover letter writing workshops are offered at most law schools, and some go so far as to offer videotaped practice interviews with critique by experienced advisers. Some provide alumni advisers, particularly for esoteric fields, and many continue their services to all alumni.

Typically, the career services offices do not work with first year students until the end of their first semester or the beginning of their second. The reason is that students need time to settle in to legal education before they start the job search. As a practical matter, the office is typically so preoccupied with second and third year on-campus interviewing during the fall semester, that any first year student would get short shrift. It also makes sense that summer employers will want to see at least one semester of grades before they hire you for the summer, if they are planning to hire any first year students at all.

EVOLUTION OF INTERESTS

"A funny thing happened to me on my way to the ACLU...I discovered Tax Law (or Bankruptcy or Employment or some other specialty)" is a familiar refrain heard throughout my career. I used to quip that 50 percent of incoming students wanted international law, 50 percent wanted entertainment law, and 50 percent wanted environmental law as a career.

Once you begin your legal studies, reality sets in and your interests develop or change. My best advice to you is not to fight this, but to embrace it. Your courses may alter your career goals and interests, as may your extracurricular activities. You may be influenced by an experience as a research assistant, an internship or pro bono placement, a summer job, or reading a book in or out of class. Your three years in law school are your opportunity to expose yourself to as wide a range of subject areas and areas of practice as you can imagine. If you follow your heart in this exploration, you have the best chance of finding at least a good match in your career. Make attending whatever panel discussions, workshops, and alumni gatherings your school offers part of your schedule, picking up as much information as you can along the way. It may help you avoid mistakes that would divert you from your path to career satisfaction.

SUMMER EMPLOYMENT

In the second semester of your first year, you may experience your first on-campus interviewing opportunity. Depending on the demand for first year law students by firms, you may find it easy to find employment through this mechanism. Your attractiveness to law firms may also depend on your experience prior to law school. Students who have been consultants or investment bankers, or who have extensive experience in any number of fields will have the best shot at the jobs available for the first year summer.

Statistically, the easier you find it to be employed through this program, the less likely you are to look at other options. The silver lining to not finding a high paying firm job in your first summer is that you are more likely to try some other alternatives and to develop some job searching techniques beyond presenting good grades and scores and passable interviewing skills. This could serve you well in the long run.

The summer after the first year is the most convenient time to explore a public service career. You may find an opportunity as a government or judicial intern, or as a volunteer (or very low-paid worker) in a nonprofit or NGO. Even if you work as a volunteer, it is a good investment of your time if you want to explore this avenue. You may be more likely to be paid, or to be attractive as a volunteer, if you have some previous experience or expertise to offer. If you have volunteered during the academic year for a particular organization, you could be first in line for a paid position. If you have a pro bono requirement at your school, consider fulfilling it during your first year, and it may also serve as your volunteer opportunity. They don't need the training time and effort if you are ready to hit the ground running. Some schools, including HLS and NYU, encourage this exploration by offering summer grants to students seeking public service employment during the first summer. Other schools, even if they do not offer grants, will dispense with the requirement that students contribute to their education from summer earnings.

If you are not interested in exploring public service work, and the on-campus interviewing program does not lead to a job, seek to build on what you have done in the past, adding a legal component, as you prepare to market yourself for more general opportunities. If you are interested in staying in the same city where your law school is located, seek a research assistantship with a faculty member, or do the same at a law school near your home, or wherever else you hope to spend the summer. Consider going far from home and school if opportunity knocks. It provides the opportunity to experience another part of the country. Another alternative, available mostly to students with foreign language ability and experience living in other countries, is a summer internship in a foreign law firm. English speaking countries are open to all, but fluency in a foreign language will facilitate your going wherever that language takes you. HLS has a program where students interested in this option begin their search late in the first term of law school and have a host of alumni offered opportunities to choose from. Other schools with large international alumni populations and/or study abroad programs may offer the same.

SECOND SUMMER: THE ON-CAMPUS INTERVIEW: CONVENIENCE OR A TRAP?

If it is ever going to be easy for you to find a job in the legal profession, the first semester of your second year is the time. If you are at one of the top or second tier law schools, law firms will participate in an on-campus interviewing program at your school. To satisfy their demand for new lawyers, law firms have focused on students who have completed their first year. Competition is such among the firms that they seek to have a large number of participants in their summer program, which becomes a try-out for a permanent position. Again, depending on the year and the demand for new associates at the firm, many to most summer associates will be made an offer to join the firm after graduation. Students who seek and are offered a judicial clerkship can take up the offer after completing the clerkship.

The on-campus interview program cuts two ways. For those who want to explore working for large or medium-sized corporate firms, it is a great convenience to have the firms come to the school to conduct initial interviews. The student needs only to prepare a resume, dress as a professional, and show up for twenty-minute interviews. The firms invite those students in whom they are most interested to visit the firm for a day. Known as "call-backs," these visits are largely for recruiting, although not everyone receives an offer from a particular firm. However, many students will receive multiple offers, and will have the opportunity to decide which firm they will join. Some students can split their offers, spending half the summer at one firm and half at another. Sometimes the split is between a firm and a public service organization or between two offices of the same firm in different cities.

For those students who are pretty sure they don't want to work at a big or medium-sized firm, the on-campus program feels like a trap. The money is so good and the firms so eager to hire, that only the rare person completely shuns the process. Those who do may be ambivalent about "missing the boat." There are good arguments for the value of knowing what goes on in these firms even if you have no intention of making a career with them. If your career goal is to work in the public service or in the government, the argument is that you need to know how the "enemy" thinks. Besides, what you earn during your second summer can really help to finance your third year of law school, reduce your future debt burden, etc.

Most firms make every effort to give the summer associates a good time, not working them too hard and having exciting social events as a part of the experience, and students may well be lulled into thinking that the summer experience is a true reflection of what it will be like after graduation. It is easier to start at a large firm and then move to a smaller firm or another area of practice than to do the reverse, and the second summer is where you first make that decision. If you go this route, keep in mind the cultural fit and the areas of practice and work to match your interests and personality with the firms which make you offers.

JUDICIAL CLERKSHIPS

Judicial clerkships are a popular choice after law school, particularly for those students who have done well in law school, and who want to keep open the option of teaching law at some point in their careers. Clerkships, especially at the federal level, are a prestigious form of continued legal education. They offer the opportunity to do research and writing, to work under supervision of a judge, who in most cases is an experienced jurist. They present the opportunity to see what goes on in court from the judge's side of the bench and to possibly have an influence on the judge's decision.

The most desirable clerkships are in the federal courts, and some who have served these clerkships have the opportunity to serve in the most prestigious of clerkships, for a Justice of the United States Supreme Court. Students from the top law schools have the greatest opportunity to serve at the federal level, and the positions are in high demand. State courts are the next most attractive, with the highest court in each state attracting the strongest applicants.

JOINT DEGREE PROGRAMS

The attainment of an additional degree, through a joint or concurrent degree program, does not necessarily increase your employment opportunities. They may help to focus your job search. If you intend to go into government law, a corporation, or the nonprofit sector, the additional skills you gain in a public policy program or from an MBA program may help you to find a good match in that direction. At the same time, the added education can send mixed signals to the large corporate firms about where your true interests lie.

FURTHER LEGAL EDUCATION—THE LL.M. AND SJD

For most students, the JD is a terminal degree, and immediate continuing education means a clerkship. Later in life, you may participate in continuing legal education programs, but nothing leading to a degree. For a small number of JD students, however, continued legal education in the form of an LL.M. or SJD degree is an attraction. For the most part, Americans limit their quest to the LL.M. degree, and most of the candidates for the SJD (or JSD) degree are foreign lawyers for whom the degree is like a PhD in law, and will enable them to teach law, or become judges, in their home countries.

The most common LL.M. degree sought by Americans is in Taxation, and numerous schools have substantial LL.M. programs in this field. Most of the other candidates for the LL.M. degree are foreign lawyers, although some Americans from the lower level law schools do seek the LL.M. to enhance their credentials for the law teaching market.

FINAL THOUGHTS

Whatever road you take out of law school, consider the various directions in which it may lead, and what your alternatives will be after your first job. Seek the advice of the career services professionals, your faculty mentors, your alumni advisers, and other members of the profession whose advice you trust. You may have to choose between following conventional wisdom or rejecting it to follow your own heart.

EPILOGUE

Some Final Thoughts

THE SPAN OF TIME you will devote to applying to law school is extremely short in the context of your education and your career. It can be a very stressful but ultimately rewarding experience.

The preparation for your law school application and legal education began early in life when you likely did not even have the goal in mind. Very few people make all the right choices along the way to gain maximum advantage, and it is always possible to make up for digressions or even having lost your way. Preparation for any career is incremental. Everything you have done before you apply feeds into the law school experience, and what you add in law school combines with that to prepare you for your professional life.

The best advice I can give is to take a simple, straightforward approach to your applications. Be yourself at all times, not a cookie cut into the shape you think law schools want in their students. The application process can be daunting when you think of all that goes into it and the importance of what comes back. Take it one step at a time, focusing on each component separately, but then review the whole for consistency and cohesion. The whole should be worth more than the sum of the parts.

Even if you follow closely every piece of advice I offer, you may be disappointed in your choice of schools. Remember that a good legal education is achievable at any accredited law school. After your offers of admission are in hand, take a moment to reflect and realize that you can make the most of the opportunities you have and turn your accomplishments, wherever they are achieved, into a solid launching pad for a very successful professional career. The journey is as important as the goal, and making the best match for yourself can be of as much value as—or more valuable than—getting into the best law school.

I wish you the very best in your quest for a legal education and a very successful career!

REFERENCES

Chapter 3:
1. Light, Richard J., *Making the Most of College*, Harvard University Press, 2001. p. 53.
2. Ibid, p. 45ff.
3. Ibid, p. 54.
4. Ibid, p. 63–65.
5. Ibid, pp. 66–69.
6. Ibid, p. 35ff.
7. Ibid, p. 28.
8. Ibid, p. 29.

Chapter 5:
1. www.abanet.org/legaled/statistics
2. Osborn, John Jay, Jr., *The Paper Chase*, Whitson Publishing Co. 1970. A novel, turned film, that dramatizes the author's first year at Harvard Law School.

Chapter 18:

1. www.abanet.org/legaled/statistics
2. Tuition and living expense figures are from individual school web sites for the year 2007–08, and typically increase each year.
3. Heather Wells Jarvis, *Financing the Future, Responses to the Rising Debt of Law Students, 2nd Edition, 2006.* Equal Justice Works, pp. 17–18.
4. Ibid, p. iv.
5. *2006 Public Sector and Public Inters Attorney Salary Report,* National Association of Law Placement.
6. Wilder, Gita, *Law School Debt Among New Lawyers—After the JD Monograph, 2002,* National Association of Law Placement.
7. National Association of Law Placement press release, August 1, 2006.

GENERAL READING

Two books that I consider very helpful to an aspiring professional are listed below. The first, by Alan Dershowitz, will be helpful as you think about the particular issues that lawyers encounter. The second, by Howard Gardner, is a wonderful conceptual guide to your overall preparation in school and as you prepare for a professional career.

1. Dershowitz, Alan, *Letters to a Young Lawyer,* Basic Books, 2001.
2. Gardner, Howard, *Five Minds for the Future,* Harvard Business School Press, 2006.

INDEX

About the Author

Joyce Putnam Curll served for eighteen years as the Admissions and Financial Aid Dean at Harvard Law School. During that time she evaluated more than 120,000 applicants for admission to the law school. Formerly she served as Director of Admissions and Admissions Dean during sixteen years at NYU Law School, where she evaluated approximately 100,000 applications. She also served on the Finalist Selection Committee for the Truman Foundation's Scholarship Program.

Dean Curll served on the Board of Trustees of the Law School Admissions Council, on the Board of Directors of Law School Admissions Services, Inc., as Chair of the Section on Pre-Legal Education and Admissions to Law School of the Association of American Law Schools, and on Accreditation Inspection Teams for the ABA. She also served as the law school liaison to the Northeast Association of Pre Law Advisors. She earned a Bachelor of Arts cum laude at Harvard University and a graduate degree in Urban Planning at New York University.